When *NO* Means *NO*

When NO Means NO

A Guide to Sexual Harassment

by Cheryl Gomez-Preston
with Randi Reisfeld

A Birch Lane Press Book
Published by Carol Publishing Group

A Birch Lane Press Book
Published by Carol Publishing Group
Birch Lane Press is a registered trademark of Carol Communications, Inc.
Editorial Offices: 600 Madison Avenue, New York, N.Y. 10022
Sales & Distribution Offices: 120 Enterprise Avenue, Secaucus, N.J. 07094
In Canada: Canadian Manda Group, P.O. Box 920, Station U, Toronto,
    Ontario M8Z 5P9
Queries regarding rights and permissions should be addressed to
Carol Publishing Group, 600 Madison Avenue, New York, N.Y. 10022

Carol Publishing Group books are available at special discounts for
bulk purchases, for sales promotions, fund-raising, or educational purposes.
Special editions can be created to specifications. For details, contact:
Special Sales Department, Carol Publishing Group, 120 Enterprise Avenue,
Secaucus, N.J. 07094

Manufactured in the United States of America
10 9 8 7 6 5 4 3 2 1

Library of Congress Cataloging-in-Publication Data

Gomez-Preston, Cheryl.
    When no means no : a guide to sexual harassment by a woman who won
  a million-dollar verdict / by Cheryl Gomes-Preston, with Randi
  Reisfeld.
       p.   cm.
     "A Birch Lane Press book."
     ISBN 1–55972–143–X
     1. Sexual harassment of women—United States.   I. Reisfeld,
  Randi.   II. Title.
  HQ1237.5.U6G64   1992
  305.42—dc20   92–39838
                                                          CIP

To everyone who has been blessed enough to
rise above personal tragedy

Contents

Preface

Sexual harassment didn't begin with Anita Hill. It's been around since Biblical times—there's the tale of the servant who was jailed, because he spurned the advances of his master's wife (Gen. 39: 1–20). It appears in a Louisa May Alcott story about a desperately poor young domestic who was forced to quit the job she needed to survive when she refused to sleep with her boss. Slave women were the most sexually-harassed people in history. In fact, sexual harassment has been going on so long in the workplace, it seems merely an occupational hazard to many generations.

What Anita Hill and the October 1991 Clarence Thomas confirmation hearings did was bring sexual harassment into the spotlight. A gross injustice that has too long plagued our workplaces began to be illuminated. Suddenly, it was the hot topic. Dialogues began between coworkers; everyone was talking about it and sharing experiences; each day seemed to bring another revelation from some famous person who'd once been victimized. It was an exciting beginning—but it was only a beginning.

Sexual harassment hardly ended with the Thomas-Hill hearings. But when the media moved on to the next topic on the titillation meter, sexual harassment once again was relegated into the background of our collective national consciousness. We can't let it stay there—it's much too real and much too destructive, and in the end, affects every one of us.

I should know, for I was one of the people most savagely affected. In 1977, I began my career as a police officer in Detroit, Michigan. In 1984, I filed a lawsuit against the Detroit Police Department on the grounds of sexual harassment. In 1987, a jury awarded me damages of $1.2 million, the largest settlement ever handed down for sexual harassment in Michigan state history.

My harrowing experience—on the job and in the court system—turned my life upside down and inside out. I plunged into the depths of despair, eventually to rise to a new awareness and a new purpose.

In 1988, I founded the Association for the Sexually Harassed (ASH), a nonprofit organization through which I counsel and educate other victims, as well as those who victimize; I work not only with individuals, women and men alike, but also with corporations and universities. Because of my expertise, I am routinely called on to serve as a consultant and expert in court cases involving sexual harassment.

Sexual harassment is my life's work. I took the worst possible circumstance and turned it into something positive, something that I hope will help others.

In this book I detail my own personal story and the stories of others I've worked with. I explain exactly what sexual harassment *is* and what it really does to its victims—and how it affects every single one of us whether we realize it or not. Most important, with this book you will learn what to do if it happens to you.

I am neither a lawyer nor a lawmaker, a psychiatrist nor an analyst, a scholar nor a celebrity. *But I have been there.* I know the games and I know the pain. I know all too well the toll sexual harassment takes on victims and their families. I know something else, too: *You don't have to "go along to get along."* When you say "No," it means no.

Acknowledgments

Thanks to Stacey Woolf of Bob Woolf Associates. Thanks to Hillel Black and Carol Publishing Group. Thanks for believing in this project.

There have been many things I have taken for granted in my lifetime. The most important were God and my family. The majority of my life was spent with my mother and I being angry with one another. I am grateful to Mrs. God for allowing my mother and I to resolve our problems, so that when she passed, in 1988, we were at peace with one another.

Since tomorrow is not promised to any of us, I want to take the time today to also thank: my creator for helping me endure this tragedy, the memory of my mother, Adrianne Tumpkins, and my husband and children Ben, Reagan, and Kyle, I love you, you are my reason for living.

I especially appreciate the support from my grandfather Amos Cecil Smith, Lois Goosby-Smith, Lavern Lockett, the memory of Bernice Kincaid, my dearest cousin Mona Harris-Ross, Tamara Woods, my attorney Michael Jackson, Esq., Marie Jamison, my dearest sister Kim Tumpkins, and my dear friends Sarah McMillian-Pruett and Ella Joyce.

Randi Reisfeld gratefully acknowledges the contributions of Sandra Choron, Ron Schaumburg, Maura Christopher, Michael and Laura Mandelbaum, and Margaret Schultz—thanks, everyone!

When *NO* Means *NO*

PART ONE

When No Means No

It Happened to Me

Victims cite many reasons for not reporting sexual harassment: some don't want to make waves, be demoted, gossiped about, ostracized. They need to feel a part *of* something and don't want to sever those bonds. Others don't report problems because they have always dreamed of a particular career, worked hard for it, in fact they can't imagine life without it, and are afraid they might derail it if they bring a sexual harassment issue out in the open. Finally, many victims simply need the job to survive and cannot afford to lose it—financially or emotionally—under any circumstances.

I had not one or two, but all of those reasons. When faced with sexual harassment, I did not want to recognize it, deal with it, let alone report it, and certainly not litigate it. The risk was too great. It meant losing what to me was my entire life. Becoming a police officer was more than a dream, and it was more than a way to support my family—although it most definitely *was* both of those things. Being a police officer filled a void for me that had been empty since childhood. All my life I had been searching for three things: a sense of myself, a real family, and happiness.

The Detroit Metropolitan Police Department gave me all those things.

Sexual harassment ripped it all away. And when it did, I felt like I had no life at all.

Childhood: Longing to Belong

My childhood was unhappy and chaotic. By the time I was born, on October 12, 1954, my father, Ramon Gomez, had already left my mother, Adrianne. She was very young, broke, and pregnant; he was irresponsible. My mother's bitterness toward him was redirected toward me, although I didn't know why until I was a teenager.

As a small child, I lived on the west side of Detroit with my maternal grandparents, Amos and Mildred Smith. They were kind to me, and though I knew I had a real mom, I thought of them as my parents. When I was five, my mother remarried and took me to live with her and her husband who adopted me without telling me. My mother taught me to call him "Dad," but I never really felt fatherly love or compassion from him. When my brother and sister were born, I felt even more isolated. I didn't look like either of them, who both took after their father. My brother seemed to be Dad's favorite, and my sister was definitely Mom's favorite. I was just sort of "there."

Because I felt not quite part of this family, I reacted by doing everything I could to make them love me. That sometimes included protecting them. Our neighbors were lower-middle class, but they owned their own, modest homes. It was the kind of place where folks would sit out on their front steps until midnight while the kids played in the alleyway. Although it wasn't crime-ridden, still there were rougher, older kids who picked on younger ones. Without being asked to, I always protected my brother—it was instinct. He seemed to be in trouble all the time, and I appointed myself the person to clean up his messes.

There were even situations where I protected my mother. When a group of older girls tangled with her, I was the one who came to her rescue with a baseball bat in hand. I was very outgoing, strong and athletic—I could play any sport, do anything the boys could do, sometimes better. For the most part, the neighborhood boys respected and liked me.

No matter what I did, though, and whom I did it for, it didn't help me fit in with my family, nor get the love and support I so desperately craved. I can recall only one occasion during my childhood when my mother backed me up. I was in fourth grade at St. Cecilia's, a Catholic school, and the nun, it seemed, was unaccustomed to teaching black/

hispanic children. Once, when I got up to sharpen a pencil, she scolded me, saying, "Stop acting your color." Even then, I deeply resented her comment—I marched right out of that classroom and walked all the way home. When I told my mother what had happened, she took off for the school and berated that nun in front of the class. I was so proud that day—it was the only time my mother took my part.

One day at my grandmother's house, I found a photo of an extremely handsome man standing with my mother. Instinctively, although no one had ever said otherwise, I suddenly knew my adopted father wasn't my real father, that the man in the photo was. When I confronted my mother with my discovery, my life started falling apart. I was thirteen years old.

My mother sat me down and confirmed what I already knew: the man in the photo, Ramon Gomez, was my father; he'd left both of us a long time ago. She told me I was Puerto Rican—but never to tell anyone. She was embarrassed and ashamed of that, and I should be too. She told me I should be grateful to my adopted father for adopting me.

Her confession affected me profoundly, but I wasn't grateful. I was angry with my adopted father. He'd adopted me in name, but never in his heart. I never felt so hurt in my life, or so alone. I'd always suspected I didn't belong; now I knew why.

All those years of anger and bitterness about my real father poured out of my mother and landed right on me, starting years of constant verbal and some physical abuse. Admittedly, I wasn't the most obedient of adolescents. I rarely did what I was told to without mouthing off. There were the usual generation-gap problems: I wanted to wear my hair in a big Afro, and they wouldn't let me. I wanted to pierce my ears, and they said no. The undercurrent of real animosity, however, made our problems more serious than in other teenager-parent relationships. In no uncertain terms my mother came right out and told me, "The reason I hate you so much is because you remind me of your father."

Having my adopted father around didn't help. If he'd been less than compassionate before my teen years, he was much worse during them. When I told him a friend of his was coming on to me, he said nothing. Generally, he never spoke to me, making me feel like I didn't exist. Once, however, he said words I will never forget, for they are part of what propelled me to become the fighter I am. He said, "Of the three kids in this household, I never expected you to amount to anything." He then added that I was the worst possible combination of ethnic groups, black and Puerto Rican. I was a loser now and destined to be a loser always.

For many years, I felt like a nothing. I didn't belong in the family I lived with; I was ashamed of being biracial. I wasn't allowed to tell anyone I was adopted, so I was ashamed of that too. My own biological father had thrown me away like a piece of garbage.

I ran away from home several times. Once, my adopted father and my mother actually threw me out—they shoved my clothes in a black garbage bag and kicked me out the door into the rain. My grandparents took me in. If it weren't for them, I don't know where I would have gone or what would have become of me. Through good and bad times, my grandfather has remained my one true supporter.

I had other family in Detroit, uncles and cousins whom we visited all the time. My exposure to them finally lit a fire under me and got me moving in a positive direction. My mother's family had serious drug and alcohol problems; they encouraged me to smoke marijuana and snort cocaine. Luckily I reacted badly and never became a user.

One of my most vivid early memories is of an uncle lying in a drunken stupor. I was terrified of stepping over this near-lifeless body to go to the bathroom. My cousins laughed at me. To them, this was just life as usual. One of my cousins actually shot at someone—I was in the car with him at the time.

I now recognize that through the grace of God I was able to see my family for what they were. I saw what alcohol and drugs had done. They had *nothing!* In my late teens, I made the most important decision of my life. No matter how long it took, how hard it was, if it near killed me, *I* was going in a different direction. I would not be like them. *They* were the losers. I wanted *out*.

Growing up, I used to watch a TV program called "Honey West," about a female private investigator. She was independent, strong, and self-confident, exactly what I wanted to be. When I was trying to figure out what to do with my life, I thought about those qualities and suddenly it came to me: I wanted to be a police officer. It would save me from becoming a substance abuser and criminal like most of my family. In fact, I'd be just the opposite: I would enforce the law. I knew, too, police officers shared a strong cameraderie, a strong sense of family and loyalty. They protected one another, stuck together, and fought for one another. I wanted to join *that* family. And I knew I could do it. I wasn't college educated, but I was smart, athletic, deeply committed, and you couldn't find anyone more motivated!

My family and friends ridiculed my decision. They knew my family history, my own problems with running away, and my own run-ins with the police. They said I would never cut it.

But none of that deterred me. I applied to the police academy in 1974 when I was 19 years old. It was three years before I was accepted, during which time I worked at a variety of jobs—and wouldn't you know it, had my first experience with workplace sexual harassment. Of course, I was young, didn't recognize it for what it was, and certainly didn't know I could fight it.

My adopted father worked at a computer company—and through him, I got a job there as a machine operator. I worked with another girl and we became close friends. We both reported to the same supervisor, a black man, who began to pressure both of us to go out with him. When we resisted, he found ways to make us uncomfortable. For instance, he'd reprimand us for things like staying in the bathroom too long. When he tried to force me to sleep with him, I quit, even though I had no other job lined up, no other income, and hadn't yet heard from the police academy. Still, I decided to quit rather than put up with the constant harassment. My friend, who was white, quit as well.

When I came home and told my mother about it, her reaction was typical—*against* me. She told me that by quitting, I'd embarrassed my adopted father. It didn't matter to her that this guy was trying to force me into bed.

The Detroit Metropolitan Police Academy

The police academy finally called me up, and I entered on July 5, 1977.

For nine weeks, my class of 120 trainees was put through a rigorous physical and mental program. We worked six days a week, ten hours a day. Every morning after six thirty A.M. roll call, we ran up six flights of stairs, our books loaded in our arms, to our classroom. Anyone who took the elevator was dismissed from the academy. Physical exercise was top priority. We did sit-ups, push-ups, leg thrusts, and ran constantly. Reading and writing were also emphasized, and there were tough exams at the end of each week.

The academy was hard, but after the first week, I knew I was going to be just fine, and I relaxed. Physically and mentally I was in the best condition I'd ever been in, and I'd begun to feel really good about myself, for the first time in a long time. I made friends there. We all learned the meaning of true camaraderie; the "all for one and one for all" mentality was drummed into us. This was exactly what I'd sought.

Tactical Training Officers whipped us into shape. Sometimes their main tactic seemed to be humiliation. We were summarily called all sorts of insulting names, our relatives called even worse names! Every day we were stripped of our pride. But once they tore us down, we were "rebuilt" to be part of the system. If you didn't have the character and skills to be a police officer, either you were asked to leave, or you dropped out.

I had what it took, in every way. On September 5, 1977, I graduated—twelfth in my class. I was proud. Finally, I'd accomplished something to feel proud of. Already, I felt part of the Detroit police force family. I loved it, I lived it, I ate it up. Every breath I'd take from now on would be for my brothers and sisters in blue.

As I'd come to expect, my family did not share my enthusiasm or pride for making it onto the force. On graduation day, my classmates had many relatives to cheer them on. I had—as usual—only my granddaddy at the ceremony. It was enough. He beamed with joy as Detroit Mayor Coleman Young and Police Chief William Hart handed me my badge and diploma.

Proving Myself at the 13th Precinct

I knew when I was called up to the police academy in 1977 that the top brass had been pressured that year to balance the police force in terms of race and gender. I filled both quotas perfectly.

What I didn't know was how resentful that would make the men on the force. No one could have prepared me for what I would face once work actually began. And even if someone *had* tried to warn me, I wouldn't have listened. I felt, whatever's coming my way, there's nothing I can't handle.

I was assigned to the 13th Precinct, "the red-light district," peopled with prostitutes and pimps of all sexual orientations, plus the usual assortment of armed robbers and other criminal types. There were halfway houses, drug deals going down on every street corner, and at least one homicide per weekend.

All of which seemed, at times, easier to handle than what went on *inside* the precinct. As I said, women weren't exactly welcomed. The very first day we walked through the door, a white male cop greeted us: "Go back where you came from." I didn't know if he was referring to our rookie status, race, or gender, but I let it roll. I looked him squarely in the eye and spoke for the group: "We're here to stay." And that was that. For the moment, anyway.

We pioneered the way for women in the Detroit police force. I was one of the first women assigned to street patrol. I loved it. It was a great way to become an expert in my precinct, and I got to meet and understand the street people. After a while, I even earned their respect and a nickname—Sunshine.

I became a Jill-of-all-trades, doing all manner of street patrol, from ticketing illegally-parked cars, to standing on street corners posing as a prostitute, to buying liquor without an ID, and busting illegal gambling clubs. At twenty-two years old, I found all this exciting and fun.

Most of the male officers I was paired with did not share my enthusiasm. Some were wary, others downright resentful and let it show. I saw it as a challenge. In almost every case, I was eventually able to win their respect, and sometimes even their friendship. I learned a lot from many of my male superiors, both black and white, and I was grateful.

Although none of the women on the force were welcomed, after a while it became clear that life would be a bit easier for white women. Few of them were assigned to on-foot detail, and those who were graduated quickly to the more comfortable, more prestigious scout cars or were transferred to inside duty. Black women police officers walked the beat longer and more frequently. I noticed it but refused to let it bother me.

I also observed a level of corruption among police officers that I wasn't prepared for. Some cops consorted with prostitutes, openly and freely. Some stole equipment from the department. Although I didn't participate, I never reported anyone. After all, this was my new family—even if they weren't perfect, I would stand up for them.

After only a few weeks on the job, I encountered my first homicide—as well as the first openly hostile signs of harassment. I was paired with an older white officer, and we were dispatched to a possible shooting at a convenience store. When we got there, I found the victim, a black woman, twenty-two years old, lying behind the counter, her head half blown off. It was hard to imagine that an hour before, this had been a living human being, someone's daughter, sister, maybe someone's mother. Revulsion and nausea swept over me and I could not suppress my own thoughts of mortality. But I was a police officer. It was my duty to take control of the situation and restore order.

I yelled to my partner that I'd found the victim. Together, we took all the proper steps: called in superiors, detectives, the right bureaus, and did the paperwork.

Several other scout cars came in to assist us. Then, out of the blue, one of the officers looked at me and announced to everyone else, "Look at that dumb bitch. She is going to fuck everything up. She doesn't know what she's doing. They don't belong on this job." My partner told me to ignore him, and outwardly, I did. But I never forgot the comment.

Nor did I forget the next sexually-related incident. After completing beat duty, I was assigned a scout car and paired with an older white sergeant. I was driving when, after about a week together, he casually mentioned that he had dreamed that he and I had an affair. I hit the brakes, and told him indignantly that it wasn't a dream, it was a nightmare—further, it wasn't going to become a reality. Soon after that, he assigned me out of his car and onto scooter training.

In neither of these cases did I know the phrase "sexual harassment." Even if I had, I would not have connected it to those two incidents. Like most women in male-dominated fields, I just felt they were part of the game. As long as I didn't really have to play along, I would be just fine.

My love for the job only grew stronger, and it was reflected in my increasing competence. I rose through the ranks at the 13th Precinct and was offered many different positions. My supervisors knew I could handle them. I was the first black female officer in the history of the precinct to ride a scooter, as well as the first black female officer at the 13th to work on Community Operations Patrol, which was basically public relations. I enjoyed it and, once again, learned a lot. I also worked undercover in Internal Affairs for a brief period.

I felt I was helping people, and that felt good. And furthermore, knowing that I *could* learn and achieve gave an enormous boost to my self-esteem.

Falling in Love

Something else in my personal life added to my sense of self-worth and happiness—I fell in love with Bennett Preston.

I'd known Bennett ever since we were both students at St. Cecilia's elementary school. He was tall and handsome—the first boy in our class to get peach fuzz on his upper lip. I didn't much like him back then. Bennett was the teacher's pet, a really studious, serious type who always had the right answer and wouldn't let anyone sneak a look at his paper during an exam. At that point in my life, I was more attracted to the popular, social, and athletic crowd. Which isn't to say that I was what we called "fast." Starting in junior high and then high school, the really popular girls got a reputation for "giving it up." That wasn't me. The nuns had drilled fear into my heart so completely, I thought that if I even let a boy kiss me I would go straight to hell.

When St. Cecilia's closed in 1969 Bennett and I went our separate ways, I to Cass Technical High School, he continuing at parochial high school and then on to college and medical school.

In 1979, he was in med school, doing a rotation at Detroit Receiving Hospital (the county facility that took indigents), when, one day, I arrested a mentally disturbed felon and escorted him to the hospital for admittance.

If I could have chosen the day on which to meet my future husband, it wouldn't have been that one. Just before bringing him in I'd scuffled with the patient—and I looked it. My shirt was wrinkled, my hair was a mess. Still, it didn't stop me from noticing the tall, attractive med student down the hall—and soon I recognized him.

Bennett and I clicked right away. We had a lot to catch up on—we hadn't seen each other in ten years. We became good friends first, found we could talk to each other about anything and everything, and finally we fell in love. At twenty-four, I'd had some experience with men; not a lot, but enough to know that the kind of love I felt for Bennett comes once in a lifetime. We found in one another true soul mates.

There was no cheering on the home front. My family was not interested in my social life; his family flat out didn't approve of our relationship. We felt we had no choice but to elope, and that's exactly what we did. We got married on July 27, 1979.

We knew our life together wasn't going to be easy at first. Aside from the parental disapproval, we didn't have much money. Bennett was in medical school—although he was moonlighting at night, he had little income. We felt we could live on my salary—just under three hundred dollars a week—if we were very, very careful.

Put to the Test

Life on the job became dicier, but as always, I felt up to the challenge. The press was debating whether women police officers really could physically handle the street, whether they provided effective backup for their male partners in dangerous situations. The articles angered me. I knew what serving as someone's partner really meant: it had less to do with physical strength than heart and soul and the ability to cover someone else's back, day in and day out. I would have given my life for my partner, as would any of the female officers I knew. We had what it took, but it was going to take a long time before we could convince many of the men.

The first time my bravery was put to the test in a dangerous situation was when a male rookie froze. We were defusing a domestic dispute in which several family members were involved. All of them were drunk, and one had a knife. When the situation seemed calm and we were about to leave, I heard one of the women yell from upstairs that she was about to stab someone. I rushed up, assuming my partner was behind me. He wasn't—he'd panicked—and *I* was the one who got stabbed in the arm.

That should have helped put to rest the fear that women officers weren't as brave as men: in many cases, we were braver. Of course, it did nothing to change attitudes, as the next two incidents prove.

This time, I was with a male who *hated* being paired with a woman and couldn't wait to show it. Late one night, we were sent to investigate a possible breaking and entering in progress at a store. As we pulled up, we heard some noise coming from inside. In many situations like this, the male partner in a coed crew would go in first, with the female providing backup. Personally, I had no problem being the first one in since I was senior to him. No problem. I went in with my flashlight—and suddenly, the noise just stopped. I turned around to check with my partner, who should have been right behind me, but he wasn't there! I was petrified. I raced back outside and found my partner sitting in the scout car. He had never come in at all. Other police cars began to arrive (it's routine to call for assistance in these situations). When they found out I'd entered the store alone, they scolded *me*.

On yet another occasion, when I was paired with this same officer on an armed-robbery run, I found myself alone and vulnerable when handcuffing a suspect. Again, my partner *never came inside* to back me up. He just sat in the scout car and said, "You don't belong on this job; women belong at home. You want to do this job? Do it by yourself." Once again, other scout cars came to assist yet no one bothered to reprimand my partner.

This time, I spoke to my lieutenant and reported all three incidents in detail. I added that I didn't want to work with either the rookie or the other officer ever again. His response was, basically, "Too bad. You'll work with whomever I say." I stood up to him and told him that I didn't know what kind of games he was playing here, but he wasn't going to play with my life. I threatened to file a complaint. But when push came to shove, the witnesses I had refused to corroborate, and everything got swept under the rug.

I was punished for bringing the complaint. I was taken out of scout car patrol and put back on the street beat. No action was ever taken against either of the male officers. I was angry at the gross injustice— still, I accepted my fate. As it turned out, I wouldn't be on foot patrol very long this time.

Getting Laid Off

Although we knew our early married life would be a struggle financially, Bennett and I agreed that we wanted children right away.

To both of us, family was the most important thing in our lives. Bennett had lost his real mom when he was only seven and longed to have a family of his own. When I got pregnant soon after our marriage, we were both thrilled.

At work, as soon as I started to show, I was transferred to desk duty.

Our daughter, Reagan Preston, was born on April 24, 1980. Bennett and I were ecstatic. She was an eight-pound, four-ounce, bright-eyed beauty, a true testament to our love. She made us a family.

As soon as my maternity leave was up, I went back to work. Since Bennett was still in medical school, we really had to rely on my salary. Getting him through med school was our number one priority; we didn't want anything to stand in the way of that goal. Sometimes I drew night duty and could spend my days with Reagan, while Bennett was there for her at night. When we were both at work, my mother cared for her, then her only grandchild.

I had been back only a few months—it was just after working security detail for President and Mrs. Reagan at the Republican Convention—when I, along with twelve hundred other police officers, was laid off. According to Mayor Young, there was no money in the Detroit budget.

There was no money in our household either. I went on unemployment and collected a grand total of one hundred dollars per week. Even though Bennett worked longer hours at the hospital, we couldn't make the rent. We moved to what was called a Section Eight housing project, where rent was paid based on a sliding scale of what you could afford.

It was tough, but I didn't stand still. I got a part-time job at the suburban Royal Oak Police Department, during the fall of 1980. The atmosphere there was completely different from the 13th Precinct, but I was determined to adjust to it. I was paid according to the number of hours I worked, which was at the complete discretion of the lieutenant in charge.

This man had been accustomed to getting his way with the female officers—until he came across me. When I refused to sleep with him, he cut my hours until I earned almost nothing. Once again, I was angry and frustrated, but I didn't know I could do anything with those emotions besides fume.

Luckily, just as my hours were cut at Royal Oak, I heard that another suburban department was hiring, and in 1981 I got a position on the Inkster Police Force. Things went smoothly there until I became pregnant again. I became the first woman officer there to be in that situation. They didn't know what to do with me. As it turned out, this pregnancy was medically difficult (I came close to losing the baby), so I had to take more time off than was generally allotted. The department used that as an excuse to give me leave without pay. But I had a wonderful supervisor who urged me to challenge the discharge as unlawful, and with the help of an attorney, I was able to collect disability.

Then, three incredible things happened, all on the very same day, April 13, 1982. I was officially laid off from the Inkster Police Department; my son Kyle was born; *and* I got notice that I was officially *rehired* at the Detroit Police Department.

I couldn't know that after all I'd been through up to this point, my troubles were just beginning.

"You Don't Need This Job—And We're Gonna Make Sure You Leave, Bitch"

It looked like smooth sailing ahead. Bennett had finally graduated from medical school, done his internship, and was starting his residency. He would only be making eighteen thousand dollars a year, but added to my salary, it was a big step for us. We felt we had two incomes at last and would soon be on our feet. We made all sorts of plans: to pay off all our bills, buy a home, and start to reap the benefits of all our hard work and sacrifice.

When I returned to the Detroit police, in July 1982, I didn't go back to the 13th Precinct but instead was transferred to the 15th. It was in an area that was still predominately white—and known for racial tension. That tension was felt outside as well as inside the precinct. The moment I walked through the door on that very first day, before a word was said, or a look exchanged, I felt it in the pit of my stomach. I brushed the anxiety aside, even though I knew gut reactions are generally the truest.

I reported to the precinct's commanding officer, who was black and seemed to want to give me a fair shake. He told me he had an open-door policy and that I should feel free to come in anytime to discuss any problems. He also asked if I was happily married. The question seemed out of context, but, innocent enough. Looking back, I think he knew I was going to have a lot of problems, and quickly.

Word had spread of my arrival before I actually got there. The police officers were not only informed that a black woman was coming, but also that she was married to a doctor. Those facts pushed a lot of buttons within the precinct: there were racists who were prepared to dislike me; there were misogynists who didn't trust female officers; and there were others who plainly felt: "She doesn't need this job. She's married to a doctor. She's taking it away from a laid-off male who has a family to support." All these people made their feelings known, and quickly. It didn't matter that Bennett was just a resident and not making much money, that my salary was crucial to our survival. It mattered less that I was competent, experienced, and loved being a police officer.

During my first week at the 15th Precinct, a lieutenant told me straight up, "I don't like you, and I'm putting you on notice: I'm going to be looking for reasons to write you up [report you]."

His words were punctuated by those of two other officers, who during my first week on the job, told me, "We're going to do one of three things: make you quit, get you fired, or see to it that you get hurt out on the street." I was shaken this time, and bewildered. What had I done to be treated so contemptuously?

I tried hard to ignore them all and just do my job. But they weren't about to let it rest. One day, a couple of white supervisors showed up at my home. When the housekeeper (who helped my mother with the kids) refused to let them in, they tried to push past her. They asked if I really lived there, if my husband lived there too, was he black or white, and did we own the house? Although the housekeeper was smart enough not to answer, they'd made their point. They knew where I lived, and wanted me and my family to feel vulnerable. After seeing the housekeeper, they decided their assessment of my being rich was right on: I didn't really need the job, I was snooty, and their attitude was justified. I began to be more and more isolated at the precinct. Very few people would even talk to me, let alone befriend me.

I decided to avail myself of the commander's open-door policy and complain about the way I was being treated. His attitude was casual.

He said they were jealous because I was married to a doctor. Then he indicated that he would be willing to help me out... but in the same breath asked if I was really happily married; did I fool around? I got the message. I told him I'd just handle the situation on my own, without his help.

At this point, I was more angry than scared. When I calmed down, I felt that all this would soon blow over, as soon as these cops got to know me a little better. Then they'd see what a good and loyal officer I was: they'd forget about Bennett's medical degree; and the jealousy would fade away. I was naive!

Nothing faded away. In fact, it got much, much worse. The verbal taunts escalated and racial epithets followed. Insulting notes were left in my locker or on my desk. Some of the messages were "Go back to Africa," "Nigger bitch," "Die bitch," "Rich bitch," "Spic bitch." I was angry and upset but not really shaken by this sophomoric display. But then the death threats began, and that was truly frightening.

I knew I had to confront the commander again. I felt that once I showed him the racial epithets and death threats, he would have to take me seriously.

"Sleep With Me, or Else"

The commander's attitude shocked me more than anything my co-workers were doing: he was completely cavalier about the situation, even after seeing the death threats. "This is the mentality of the white boys over here," he told me. He showed me a porno magazine centerfold, a picture of a naked woman, with the words *Kiss ass, nigger* written on her genitals. "See this?" he said. "This was in another officer's locker." A black male patrol inspector, too. Here I was, standing there, looking at this black commanding officer, and he was making excuses. My uneasiness returned.

Then the commander reverted to his theme about my marriage. I realized that even at this level of seriousness, he would do nothing to help me.

Although no one had advised me to do so, in October 1982 I started to document everything that was happening to me. I included the harassment incidents in my daily reports. When my superiors told me to rewrite them and leave out the harassment, I did as I was told; but when my original reports were thrown in the garbage, I retrieved them. I didn't know why at that point—something just told me to do that.

Things got progressively worse. The male officers continued to harass me. I was poked in the breasts and grabbed in the buttocks, almost routinely. They stole my equipment, which I had to report as missing—which meant I'd be written up. Never in my entire career had I ever been written up before. And I certainly wasn't misplacing my equipment.

I decided to talk to my union steward, to show him the racial epithets and death threats and report the commander's conditions for his assistance. The union man's advice was to stay out of the commander's way—as if I could! He went on to inform me that in *his* opinion, I was "a lazy broad who had no business being on the police force." Clearly, there would be no help from that end.

On a Saturday afternoon several weeks later, I reported to work and was told the commander wanted to see me in his office. I was shocked—mainly because no commander ever came in on a Saturday. I couldn't imagine what he wanted to see me about, but in about five minutes, he made it perfectly clear. The shades in his office were drawn and the door was closed. I asked why he'd come in on a Saturday, and he answered, "To get into mischief—but you don't get into that kind of mischief, do you?" I knew exactly what he meant. He continued, "It should be obvious that I want to sleep with you, and you should be flattered. I don't make it a habit to sleep with the women at the precinct. But you're different. I want to take you to bed." The only thing I could think to counter with at that moment was to remind him he was married. He just laughed. I got angry all over again and told him I had absolutely no intention of sleeping with him. I wasn't interested and never would be. I asked him what kind of a black man he was, to treat his wife and women so disrespectfully.

He said this: "Cheri, you better realize this. You've been having problems and I could help you. But if you won't cooperate, know this: if I can't fuck you one way, I'm gonna fuck you another." With that, he told me to get the hell out of his office.

In a Dark Alley at Three A.M.—Alone With an Armed Assailant

At three A.M., one frigid January night in 1983, five months after I joined the 15th Precinct, it all came to a very ugly head. I was the only woman on the street. I wasn't wearing my protective gear—did the other officers know that? They knew so much about me, I have to wonder.

A patrol car was chasing a man who had just tried to shoot someone while committing armed robbery. I was the type of police officer who would always go and back up someone, even if he wasn't my partner. I barely knew this one, but I still considered the police department my family. My partner and I were driving parallel to the chase, but when six other officers began to chase the suspect on foot, I jumped out and joined them.

I was so intent on catching the man, I didn't notice when we turned and ran into a dimly-lit alley. All of a sudden, the suspect stopped and turned. I looked over my shoulder for my backup—but no one was there. They had left me there alone, possibly to die.

I'll never forget the look on the suspect's face—he was scared. He wanted to escape, but I was blocking his way to freedom. He fumbled around the waist of his pants, trying to find his gun. I knew he was going to shoot me. I thought about my kids, my two babies at home. No way was I ready to die. I pulled my gun and fired twice, and although I didn't hit him, he fell to the ground. Within twenty seconds, officers came running from wherever they'd been. No one said a word. They didn't have to—they said it all when they abandoned me in a dark alley with an armed assailant. The ultimate death threat had been made.

I was deeply shaken and didn't know what to do. There was no point in going to the commander. I did talk to one of the few friends I had at the precinct, a black sergeant who told me bluntly I'd better get out. These guys were out to get me; hadn't I gotten the message by now? He offered to put in a transfer for me to his public relations department. It would have been a good move, not only for me, but for the department; I had experience in public relations. The commander didn't agree, and instead appointed someone with absolutely no experience there. I next requested a transfer to another precinct altogether; it was approved by everyone except my commander.

Soon, the whole thing began to feel like a never-ending nightmare. My other so-called friends on the force started pulling away from me; it just wasn't very smart to be associated with me. My whole situation felt like a time bomb ready to explode. I started to unravel—which is exactly what had been intended all along. No one understood.

Bennett didn't understand why I didn't just quit; at that time his salary alone could have sustained our family. But I simply wasn't a quitter. Cops don't quit. My sense of identity, my self-worth was tied up in being a cop—and cops don't whine and cry. I stopped talking to Bennett about my work. As the lines of communication were severed, new tension within our marriage developed, and for a long time, we fought over the smallest things.

I had to force myself to get up and go to work, and every night I'd look in on the sleeping kids, wondering if I'd make it home safely that night. Wondering if I'd ever see them again.

A Broken Foot Is a Small Price to Pay for My Life

It was a no-win situation. I couldn't stomach being at work, but I couldn't see any way out of it, and the urge to get out was becoming overwhelming. Since I wouldn't quit, I devised another way. Looking back, I know how crazy this was—but I *was* crazy; I'd been driven crazy. I decided to break my foot. I remember thinking it would just take a second and then I'd be out of there, on disability. A broken foot was a small price to pay for leaving with my life.

I picked up an old, heavy typewriter, stuck my foot out, closed my eyes, turned my head, and threw the typewriter down on it as hard as I could. The pain was excruciating; it shot up my body like a lightening rod. Tears in my eyes, I limped to the front desk and told the desk supervisor I thought my foot was broken. He smirked and said, "As soon as someone becomes available, we'll get you to the clinic." I had to wait for about 2 hours until someone "became available."

I was relieved of duty for six weeks, with disability pay. During that time away, I came to another decision. I had to report the entire situation to Internal Affairs: all the incidents of harassment *and* lodge a specific complaint against the commander. No one had ever done that before. He was the fifth highest-ranking officer in the Detroit Police Department. He was powerful and well liked. I knew I'd be risking my career, but I knew what I had to do.

The Internal Affairs division was on the sixth floor at another building. I went up, spent several hours lodging my complaint, produced evidence and took all the proper steps. Everything was supposed to be kept in confidence, but the officer in charge I spoke to happened to be a good friend of the commander. By the time I stepped off the first-floor elevator, the entire precinct knew all about my visit to Internal Affairs. The word was out: I was a traitor, a whistle-blower. If I was isolated before, I was a downright pariah now.

Hitting Rock Bottom

Internal Affairs handled my situation by transferring me, at my request, to my old stomping grounds, the 13th Precinct. This was the place where I'd done so well, made so many friends. Even though justice was not served—the commander and the offending officers hadn't been punished in any way—I thought the nightmare was finally over for me.

I returned to a new 13th Precinct. Times had changed and so had everyone's perception of me. I walked in the door branded a troublemaker. The officers there were prepared to hate me, and they did. I felt more alienated and isolated than ever.

Sexual harassment almost always takes a physical toll, and I didn't escape that part of the syndrome. I would have crying spells; I started to lose my hair; eventually my menstrual cycle completely stopped. I had bouts of depression to the point where I would come home and stay locked up in my room. I had blackout spells, so I stopped driving. One day, after buying an item in the grocery store, I became so confused I just gave the cashier a wad of money and told her to take out whatever I owed. I even began to have chest pains.

Still, I continued to report to work. Until one day, it all seemed to collapse, all at once.

The pains in my chest were so bad, I thought I was about to have a heart attack. I told the supervisor at the desk, and he just told me to go change into my uniform. I was so out of it I actually did. When I returned to the desk, the desk supervisor started yelling at me in front of everyone. He said there was nothing wrong with me and that I was trying to pawn off my problems on the police department. I became incoherent. Suddenly, I couldn't hear what he was saying; all I saw was his mouth moving. I unbuckled my holster and began to pull my gun out. I had to make him stop talking, make his mouth stop moving. I began to raise my gun to his mouth. Had another officer not grabbed me from behind, I might be writing this book from prison. As a consequence I was sent to the psychiatric ward and was not allowed to use a gun until October 1986.

I had truly hit bottom. I began to feel I had nothing to live for. About two weeks later while Bennett was at the hospital and the children were with my mother, when I got home, I decided there was really only one way out of this situation. Kneeling next to my bed, I reached beneath my mattress for my off-duty gun. My face was drenched with tears as I placed the gun at my temple. When I raised my head, I saw my reflection in the mirror, and I continued watching as I slowly began to pull the trigger. Scenes from my life flashed before me. Then, I saw pictures of my children. I focused on them. I saw my two beautiful babies, who still loved and needed me. Right then, I realized that everything, all the pain and trauma, was not just my problem; it belonged to the entire family. I finally realized I needed help, and I needed it fast. I put the gun down.

"What's Wrong With You Has a Name: It's Called Sexual Harassment"

Bennett helped me find a wonderful psychiatrist, Dr. Margaret Baima, who, within a week, admitted me to a psychiatric ward of Providence Hospital in Southfield, Michigan. I will never forget going there: Bennett just dropped me at the door and left. He could no longer handle the pain, and this was how he dealt with it. I felt totally alone.

I spent an entire summer hospitalized. Most of our friends had been distant while I had my problems at the police department, but when they found out I was in the psychiatric ward, with one or two exceptions, they deserted us altogether.

It was during some very intensive therapy there that, with Dr. Baima's help, I was able to start picking up the pieces and glue myself back together again. Dr. Baima told me that what had happened to me had a name: sexual harassment. I'd never heard those words before, let alone known what they meant. I came to understand that I wasn't crazy, but that what I had been through was enough to drive anyone over the edge. In fact, I wasn't the only person it had happened to. I wasn't alone, and I wasn't crazy. The relief was immense.

One day at the hospital, the doctor, Dr. Baima, asked me to make an art collage to help me express some of the anger and rage that burned inside me. I was insulted—cutting out pictures and pasting them on paper, that's something a child does! Then I thought, Okay, if they want a collage, I'll make them one they'll never forget!

I found some magazines and newspapers and ripped out pictures and words. Barely aware of what I was doing, I assembled them into a portrait. What emerged on paper shocked even me: there was death, violence, and blood, dead bodies, aborted fetuses, women who were hurt. At the top of the collage I had assembled jagged letters, like those in a ransom note: The words read: IF THERE'S A GOD, THEN WHY IS THERE ALL OF THIS? A MOTHER HELPS OTHER PEOPLE, A POLICE OFFICER HELPS OTHER PEOPLE. BUT WHO HELPS THAT PERSON WHEN SHE NEEDS HELP? WHERE IS GOD THEN?

When I looked into the collage, I began to see the real me. Lo and behold, I liked what I found. I began to realize that I was human, not a tough supercop who shouldn't cry, but a person filled with rage. Thanks to Dr. Baima, I understood that I had every right to be filled with rage.

From that rage came the light: I began to realize that in order to regain my sanity and reclaim my life, I had to make my anger work for me, and not against me. I had to make the negative into a positive. At that point I knew the only way to seek justice was to go outside the corrupt system and take the Detroit Police Department to court. I would sue, but not right away. For all intents and purposes, even though I now understand so much, I was still a nonfunctioning human being.

At first my hospitalization was accepted as a work-related nervous breakdown, and therefore I was getting paid. But after two weeks, the department psychiatrist was coerced into changing his diagnosis. On a weekend leave I'd had a fight with Bennett, and the police used it as a loophole to get out of paying me; saying that my problems were marital and *not* work-related. Therefore, they didn't have to pay me while I was hospitalized. With the help of an old friend who was a police officer, I filed a grievance with my union for disability compensation; I won, but it took two years to get it.

After my release from the hospital, I got notification to come back to work. Although a part of me *did* want to return and let them know they had not broken me, the very thought of it brought on an anxiety attack. My doctor submitted a six-page letter explaining that although I had every intention of returning at some point, I could not do it right now. The department decided that the reasons given were "insufficient."

I was terminated. The letter was signed by Police Chief William J. Hart, the same man who'd handed me my diploma and badge when I graduated from the police academy.

Bennett and I now entered one of the bleakest periods of our lives. From August 1983 to September 1985, I was out of work. For much of that time, I was unable to drive a car, I was in therapy three times a week. The children had to live with my mother because we had no money to buy groceries. Our utilities were turned off. We lost all our credit. We lived on milk and peanut-butter-and-jelly sandwiches. Our marriage was falling apart. Bennett couldn't help feeling I'd screwed things up royally. I felt I couldn't forgive him for thinking that way.

Putting the Pieces Back Together

Perhaps I needed to go through all this to find the strength to do what I knew I had to: I focused all my energy, as well as whatever strength and sanity I could summon, on my lawsuit. I started the process of trying to find a lawyer. I knocked on the doors of over a dozen lawyers before I found one who not only believed my story, but agreed to take the case on a contingency basis. After all, I had no money.

Some attorneys didn't believe me; others were downright rude. Because I was in such a precarious emotional state, I'd developed a stutter, and one lawyer yelled at me for not being able to tell my story quickly enough. Another told me flat out he could not take my case because suing the city of Detroit would wreck his political aspirations.

While I was searching for a lawyer, I went to the EEOC. But after they reviewed my case they discouraged me from filing a complaint. A friend of my mother's who worked at EEOC told me they were understaffed and I was wasting my time; she advised me to find outside counsel, which I was already doing. Clarence Thomas was the head of the EEOC at the time.

During many meetings with the lawyer who did agree to represent me, I came to terms with my real reasons for going to court: even though we were going to ask for a lot of money in back pay and damages, that wasn't my main motivator. *I* needed to tell my story publicly, to be *believed*, to be vindicated, and to see my harassers punished.

We filed the lawsuit officially on May 5, 1984. It named the Detroit Police Department, the city of Detroit, my commanding officer at the 15th Precinct, two lieutenants, and one other sergeant.

It took two and a half years before my case came to trial. During those years, with the excellent therapy from Dr. Baima and a dedicated attorney who believed in me, I started to regain my confidence. By September 1985, I'd won my case for unlawful dismissal from the Detroit police department and was reinstated with back pay. I didn't *have* to go back to work, and certainly Dr. Baima advised against it. But I just felt that I'd been booted out unfairly—I wanted to be able to leave under my terms, and I wanted my peers to see, that no matter what they'd done to me, they hadn't broken me.

I returned to the police academy on restrictive duty in 1985. Of course, everyone knew I was suing the Police Department. You can imagine the reception I got! I was completely alienated from all my co-workers. The few former friends and colleagues I had now avoided me completely and spoke to me only when they absolutely had to. If you have ever been in a position like this, you know how devastating it can be. By this time, several women were on the force; some of whom were black and had been made supervisors. But they did not ally themselves with me—by and large, they played the game and tried to be "one of the boys." When a white female lieutenant did try to be sympathetic to me, she faced harassment by the two black female supervisors who were her subordinates.

The harassment continued. It ranged from downright dangerous— I drew the worst assignments, such as working security in one of the city's worst areas without a gun (because I was still on restrictive duty because of the incident where I pulled my gun)—to just plain stupid: I had to ask for permission to use the restroom; often that was denied, so I had to climb several flights of stairs to find another one. I had to retake the state certification exam and was told I would never pass. But I did.

My mental condition improved—I knew I wasn't crazy; I knew exactly what was going on; and best of all, I knew I was taking steps to find justice. But the physical results of sexual harassment continued to take their toll. I developed stomach ulcers and had to take four weeks' leave without pay for treatment. But I came back. Armed with a huge bottle of Mylanta, I resumed my duties. They would not defeat me.

Eventually, I was transferred to yet another precinct. I was named Senior Training Officer at the 4th Precinct in October 1986. Once again, word of my arrival preceded me, and officers there were steeled for the troublemaker. The first week on the job, my tires were slashed. I announced to the entire precinct that I had already filed a lawsuit, and I would be glad to add their names to it—no skin off my back.

They retreated. While making a felony arrest, a scuffle broke out, and part of my right kneecap was shattered. It was right at this time that I got notification of a trial date. November 11, 1986, was my last day as a police officer.

The trial itself took six weeks—grueling, humiliating, painful weeks. (Later chapters cover the ramifications of taking a case like this to trial.) I won my case, and although the other side appealed, eventually I prevailed. I won the largest jury award in the state of Michigan and the largest jury award for a police officer in the country for sexual harassment. Although two of the officers named in my suit were acquitted, and one conviction was overturned in the Court of Appeals, my commanding officer was found guilty, and was given civil conviction. He is still a Detroit Police commander.

The biggest surprise came after it was all over. I didn't feel all that different. I had thought I would finally be able to close the door and move on. And while that *did* happen—Bennett was offered a position in Philadelphia, so we literally did move—it didn't seem enough. After a while, I understood why. For me, the trial and the verdict weren't enough; the door wasn't closed. I realized that the only way it would be was to use everything I'd gone through to help others.

And that is how the Association for the Sexually Harassed was born. I used part of my settlement money to found ASH, which is a nonprofit organization that counsels and supports victims of sexual harassment. We offer a speakers bureau, and consultation services for attorneys and their clients. We do whatever is required in each specific case. Sometimes victims just need to talk to others who've been through it. In other cases, we recommend strategies and even help victims find attorneys. I have worked with many trials as a consultant and as an expert. And through ASH, I have developed training workshops for companies to deal with this problem.

This has become my life's work—but not my entire life. As I found out, in therapy and in my trial, I *do* have a *real* family, not an imagined one. In his own way, and as best as he could, Bennett has been there for me. My children once saved me from suicide, and every day they fill my life with joy. Because of what I've gone through, they are very sensitive to this problem. They are good kids, bright and talented, and I feel confident that they will go out into the world as productive, healthy human beings.

Before she died, my mother came to understand the impact of being harassed and stood in my corner as well: she told me that while she drew breath, I would never be without her support again. She held to that. I now completely understand that one of the things I was always searching for was right here all along: my family.

Going through this nearly ten-year ordeal, I also found something else that was perhaps there all the time: I know who I am. I am strong and loving, a fighter, and a giver of support. It is within my family and within my sense of self that my self-esteem has been allowed to grow and flower.

Through my story, through the facts and advice I have for you, I hope to empower you in ways that I wasn't empowered.

TWO

Defining Our Terms: Is This Really Sexual Harassment?

I find it amazing and appalling that still, even after Anita Hill, 65 percent of men and women in this country do not know what constitutes sexual harassment. Yet it has, in fact, been defined in a number of ways, by our governing bodies, and by the experts. As someone who has experienced sexual harassment firsthand, and as founder of ASH, I have my own definition. After reading this chapter, there should be little doubt left in anyone's mind.

What It Is

The Supreme Court of the United States of America defines sexual harassment as unwelcome sexual advances, requests for sexual favors, and other verbal or physical contact of a sexual nature *when* 1) submission to such contact is made either explicitly or implicitly a term or condition of one's employment; 2) submission to or rejection of such conduct by an individual is used as the basis for employment decisions affecting such individual; or 3) such conduct has the purpose or effect of unreasonably interfering with an individual's work performance or creating an intimidating, hostile, or offensive working environment.

The Equal Employment Opportunity Commission (EEOC) is the federal agency that investigates all bias in the workplace. Its definition of sexual harassment is a bit simpler than the Supreme Court's (and actually predates it):

1) Making sexual activity a condition of employment and/or promotion; or
2) the creation of an intimidating, hostile, or offensive working environment.

Although those are the letter-of-the-law definitions, they still leave quite a bit open to interpretation. For instance, who decides what is "intimidating, hostile, or offensive?" What is offensive to one person may be perfectly acceptable to another.

When I set up the Association for the Sexually Harassed, I wrote my own definition, which I feel breaks it down even more specifically. According to ASH, sexual harassment is: unwelcome exposure to physical contact, pornography, sexual jokes, requests for dates, sexual favors, and demeaning comments—made by males or females—which causes an individual's environment or workplace to become intimidating, hostile, or offensive.

Having established that, I break it down even further, so there can be no doubt left in anyone's mind. Some points may seem obvious; others less so. When it is *unwelcome*, sexual harassment is:

Violation of space. Everyone has what I call his or her "space," that invisible area that is right around you. In a crowded elevator we can't help invading each other's space; we feel uncomfortable and tend not to look at each other. But when someone is sexually harassing you, he or she comes too close, invades your space *purposely,* and repeatedly.

Mental undressing. Some people call it leering; I call it "the stare." Anyone who's been a victim of it knows exactly what I mean: when someone is looking you up and down as if undressing you. No words are said, but it's enough to make you cringe.

Lewd and/or sexual remarks—talking dirty. Some people talk this way all the time and think nothing of it. In private, and to someone who doesn't consider such language offensive, it may be acceptable. But in a working environment, during business conversations, it is out of place.

Inappropriate comments of a personal/gender-defining nature. During a business discussion, a male manager asked a female colleague, out of the blue, "What color panties are you wearing?" The remark threw her off balance, which was precisely the intent.

Jokes and/or innuendos of a sexual nature. What is funny to some people is offensive to others—and again, simply doesn't belong in a place of business. The "what's the matter, can't you take a joke?" mentality is archaic, provincial, aggressive, inappropriate, offensive, and hurtful.

Graphic or degrading comments about one's appearance, dress, or anatomy. There is a big difference between admiring someone's dress and admiring the way it "hugs your hips and waist."

Name calling, catcalls, whistles. This shouldn't have been tolerated back in third grade; it simply can't be tolerated in the grown-up work world. It is abusive.

Abuse of familiarities or diminutives, such as "honey," "sweetheart," "darling," "dear," or "baby." What is sweet at home, among loved ones, is degrading in the workplace. It automatically undermines your professionalism, *demotes* you.

Sexually-suggestive gestures. This can be anything from the middle finger in the air to a pantomime of sexual activity. Never in good taste, it is completely out of place in the workplace. If it's offensive and continual, it's harassment.

Leers and suggestive looks. I.e., when someone is talking to you but staring at your breasts. Who wouldn't be uncomfortable? If women began staring at men's crotches, chances are they'd understand a lot more readily how humiliating this is. The harasser who engages in this activity is the one who finds himself—quite often— standing behind the woman who is bending over the file cabinets.

Exposure to pornography. Playboy/Playgirl centerfolds do not belong posted in the workplace. Neither do sexually-explicit photos. Not everyone has to be offended for this to be considered harassment: if *you* are offended, that's reason enough for the posters or pictures to be removed.

Sexually-explicit cards, notes, or other written correspondence. Sometimes these missives are delivered to you personally—as mine were—but in other instances, they are displayed on someone's wall for all fellow employees to see, whether they want to or not.

Being touched, rubbed up against. Sometimes, even a hand on your shoulder can be laden with unspoken threats. You know when someone merely places a friendly hand on your shoulder or if he/she has other intentions. There is a noticeable difference. Both victims and harassers know it immediately.

Fondling, pinching, hugging, tugging, or patting.

Pressure for dates. Once you have made it clear that you are not interested, consistent badgering is harassment. A co-worker or subordinate can create an offensive or intimidating environment.

Pressure for sexual favors. (usually covert rather than overt). This is always harassment, especially when the ultimatum is expressed—give in or forget about that raise/plum assignment, *or* don't give in and get hurt/fired.

Exposing genitalia. Indecent exposure is more, even, than sexual harassment—it is a crime.

Any form of sexual harassment is illegal. It is not just inappropriate and wrong—it is punishable to the full extent of the law. Sexual harassment violates federal and state civil rights under Title VII of the 1964 Civil Rights Act. It is not a law that is simply buried on the books and never trotted out for enforcement: each year, more and more cases of sexual harassment are being prosecuted—and won.

You do not have to put up with sexual harassment.

What It Isn't

Not every instance of a perceived sexual or intimate nature is harassment.

Social ineptness, simple flirting, or an awkward expression of romantic attraction is not sexual harassment.

When there is *mutual* agreement, or when the attention is *welcomed*, it is not sexual harassment.

A big question that comes up involves *socializing after work—* going out with coworkers for drinks or dinner. If you've agreed to go, and because it's taking place away from the office, does that automatically remove it from the realm of sexual harassment? The answer is no—not automatically. It depends on the stated purpose of the socializing and what happens. If your boss asks you out to dinner to discuss a business matter—or your career advancement—and the conversation *does* stick to those topics, it is not sexual harassment. If, however, the conversation veers toward the personal—or worse, the sexually explicit—it's getting into dicier territory, especially if you make it clear you're uncomfortable. My overall advice is to avoid putting yourself in that position, if it's at all possible.

One isolated incident is not sexual harassment. If a coworker or even superior asks for a date once, is turned down, and doesn't continue, he or she is not a perpetrator.

The most important determining factor in what is and isn't sexual harassment is this: *Does the behavior continue after it has been turned down/pointed out?* Does the person stop calling you "honey"? Does he or she refrain from touching your shoulder once you've said, "Excuse me, I'm uncomfortable with that"? Has the centerfold been taken down from the wall? Do the jokes and language cease in your presence? Do you feel you can do the job you were hired to do, without interference of a sexual nature?

A yes means there is no sexual harassment.

A no, unfortunately, may mean there is.

Who Is Being Sexually Harassed?

There is no profile of a "typical" victim. Initially it was surmised that people who are mild-mannered, meek, introverted, and shy fit the stereotype of someone likely to be harassed. That, however, has been proven not to be true. I certainly did not fit the stereotype: I was outgoing, strong-willed, and in a position of authority. Through my work with other victims, I have found more evidence to substantiate the claim that *no one* is exempt; *anyone* can be a victim.

That established, however, patterns do emerge when looking at the big picture of who is likely to be sexually harassed:

More women than men
More minorities than Caucasians
More single mothers than married women
More gays than heterosexuals
More high school dropouts than graduates
More women in traditionally male-dominated fields, *whether or not* those fields are blue-collar (police, firefighters, construction

workers, clerical workers, bus drivers, domestics) or white collar/ professional (corporate executives, doctors, lawyers, teachers). In fact, women surgeons and investment bankers rank among the highest on the harassment scale.

What this last category speaks to is women who are in the minority or new to a field, thereby challenging the status quo. The boys in the club don't like to open their doors to newcomers, especially when they look and act different from themselves. When forced to by law, some react badly and vent their hostility with harassment.

Certain men perceive women like myself—assertive, outgoing, and strong—as threats. Intimidation can lead to harassment: it is the only way some men can keep that woman "in her place." In fact, as you'll see when we examine who is *doing* the harassing, sexual harassment is rarely about sex. It is always about power and its misuse.

Women are not the only victims of sexual harassment. Many men have found themselves in this predicament, but they are less likely to speak out about it. Gay men are subject to harassment more than straight men, but heterosexuals who are perceived as effeminate are just as likely to encounter it. Men who are simply *gentle*, who may not want to play the "boys will be boys" back-room games, have been subject to harassment more often than those who go along with the "program."

Teenagers and children are also apt to be sexually harassed and least likely to recognize it. When a group of boys makes a lewd comment about a girl going by, that is harassment. Whenever that girl is made to feel uncomfortable about her own body, that is harassment, and unfortunately, it almost always goes unchallenged. In later chapters, I address how we can go about nipping harassment of young people in the bud in order to work toward erasing it from our society altogether.

Finally, it has been my experience that the victim is not only the actual person harassed but can be *anyone* adversely affected by the offensive conduct. Having a co-worker under attack can affect the morale and productivity of many immediate colleagues—which, in a very real sense, victimizes *them*, too.

One more crucial point needs to be made about the victim.

The victim did not cause this to happen, not by the way she dressed or acted, nor by anything she said. In much the same way that enlightened people *now* recognize that rape victims did not invite the attack because of how they dressed or acted, so it is with victims of sexual harassment. No matter what you look like, or what signals may have been inferred by another, once the victim has said "No," she has the right to be taken at her word.

Who Is Doing the Harassing—And Why

Just as there is no profile of the typical victim, so there is no composite of a typical harasser. He can be a she. She can be straight or gay, black or white, Hispanic, Asian, married or single, your immediate supervisor, or his immediate supervisor.

In nearly every instance of work place harassment, however, the harasser is exercising power over the victim. He or she may be one or two or seven rungs up on the workplace ladder. She or he is someone who can influence others in the workplace to take her side against yours. He or she can almost always affect the *financial status* of the victim. And when someone can promote you, demote you, hire or fire you, you tend to take that person very seriously indeed.

Sexual harassers have other traits in common. Many have a predator mentality, stalking their prey well before taking any action. They seek out the most conducive circumstances: places and times when there will be no witnesses to their actions. Sexual harassers work alone, and in places where they will *be* alone. In a showdown, it is often their word against yours.

Many sexual harassers are locked in denial: they refuse to believe, even when it's pointed out, that they are acting inappropriately and illegally. [They are out of touch with reality.]

In psychological terms, the harasser is likely to be someone who has a problem relinquishing power, who needs to be in control all the time, someone who is fundamentally insecure. For some perpetrators with low self-esteem, victimizing another is the only way they can feel empowered. That is why you find some people in very high positions who are harassers: they are not "allowed" to fail in the workplace, and that notion feeds a basic insecurity.

For others, of course, harassment is simply a way to preserve the status quo: he may be forced to let women into the male preserve or club, but he sure as hell doesn't have to make them comfortable. For many men, the best way to keep a woman uncomfortable and off-balance—and hopefully scare her the hell out of the club—is by using the one "power tool" he thinks he will always have over her—his sexuality.

Above all else, sexual harassment is a way to keep women, and/or subordinates, *in their place*. Through harassment, those in power devalue a woman's (again, substitute any group) role in the workplace by calling attention to her sexuality.

Despite the vast numbers of people who may possess the qualities of harassers, statistics show that less than 5 percent of people in the workforce have been pegged as perpetrators. A genuine sexual harasser is someone who continues offensive behavior, over and over again.

Statistics

Many different groups have conducted surveys on sexual harassment in the workplace. Actual numbers differ, but the basic results are clear: it happens with far too much frequency for anyone to remain complacent.

The EEOC reports a 300 percent increase over the past ten years in sexual harassment complaints.

In research done by psychologists, 50 percent of women in the workplace questioned said they had been sexually harassed. Of that number, only 22 percent told someone else about it. *None* (0 percent) sought legal recourse.

According to the U.S. Merit Systems Protection Board, within the federal government 56 percent of 8,500 female workers surveyed claimed to have experienced sexual harassment.

According to the National Law Journal, 64 percent of women in "pink-collar" jobs reported being sexually harassed.

In polls conducted by ABC News during the Thomas/Hill hearings, 33 percent of women and less than 10 percent of men said they'd experienced it.

In a report done by Fox TV, the number is 25 percent.

In my own research, I found the number to be 35 percent of women and 11 percent of men; 42 percent of black and Hispanic females, as compared to 19.4 percent of whites. Of those numbers, 50 percent do not file a complaint; of those who *do*, 75 percent wind up being fired.

According to research at the University of Illinois by Dr. Louise Fitzgerald, only 25 percent of sexual harassment cases are botched seductions. Less than 5 percent involve outward bribes or threats (where someone comes out and says, "If you do this for me, I will help you; if you don't, I will make things difficult.") The rest are assertations of power.

In a recent survey by Working Women *magazine*, 60 percent of high-ranking corporate women said they have been harassed; 33 percent more knew of others who had been. Of all these, only 40 percent told the harasser to stop, and less than 25 percent ever reported it in any official way.

THREE

The Emotional, Physical, and Financial Effects of Sexual Harassment

An often-told joke—in many variations—goes something like this: A doctor tells a patient he's got some good news and some bad news. "Give me the bad news first," says the patient. "O.K., you've got two weeks to live," says the doctor. The patient cries, "What good news could there be?" The doctor answers, "See that nurse outside? I finally fucked her."

Jokes like that have been bandied about the workplace for so many years that most people don't even think about them. They've just been accepted for generations as part of the social landscape.

Chances are you don't find them funny. Neither do I. The problem is that many do—no doubt the same people who tell you that you're "overreacting" to instances of sexual harassment, that you just can't appreciate a simple joke. They will tell you to lighten up, develop a sense of humor. They will also tell you that the mental, physical, and emotional problems you may experience due to sexual harassment are "all in your head."

They are wrong. Dead wrong.

Sexual harassment can be devastating. The effects go far beyond the specific situation at work. I know because I was there, and I know because of the dozens of people I have counseled. The damaging effects are *real*. And they are not funny.

Sexual harassment is nothing less than emotional—and oftentimes financial—rape. It is every bit as traumatic. The physical and emotional fallout suffered by victims runs the gamut from stress to full-tilt nervous breakdowns, thoughts of suicide, and even hospitalization. I wish I were, but I am not exaggerating. Although no two people react in exactly the same way, all victims go through universal stages.

Emotional Upheaval: Four Stages

Typically, when harassment first starts, you simply feel discomfort—that sick feeling in the pit of your stomach when you know something isn't right. Still, the most common first reaction, Stage One, is to dismiss it, to make excuses, and hope you're imagining it: that hand on your knee was an aberration, a mistake. You think, Maybe it's me, I'm overreacting, that's not what he intended. . . . I'm thinking off the wall. Most people try as hard as they can to pretend it isn't happening. The idea of *saying* something to the offender, of *doing* something about it, doesn't even cross your mind at this point. No one wants to make waves, especially on the basis of what is "probably" a simple misunderstanding.

Until, that is, you can no longer pretend.

As harassment continues, you typically move into Stage Two: feeling stressed and anxious at work, wondering when and if it will happen again. Inwardly, you question every move the offender makes, trying to figure out if you're being summoned to his office for business . . . or monkey business. You try to limit contact with the person, to sit as far away as you can at meetings, take longer lunches, make more frequent trips to the bathroom, possibly assign someone else to work directly with the person. It's called avoidance.

The situation has already affected your work performance. Once you have been harassed, you can never concentrate with the same effectiveness as you did before. Suddenly, a dark cloud is hovering over your head, and no matter what you try, it won't lift.

Stage Three is when it becomes difficult to even *go* to work. You may have nightmares, bolt awake in a cold sweat, wake up in the morning with knots in your stomach. By this time, of course, you know exactly why. You take sick days, and when those are used up, you force yourself to go in. The irony isn't lost on most of us: the place we used to look forward to going to is suddenly the very place we dread.

Feeling alienated from co-workers—former friends!—is also part of Stage Three. For most victims, it's hard, if not impossible, to confide in colleagues. These are still the early stages of the reaction, and at this point you do not want to rock the boat. And then you wonder, Well, who would believe me anyway? Which leads to feelings of isolation and a "me against them"—and, eventually—a "me against the world" mind-set. It is naive to think that by telling someone what's going on, he or she will take your part. Truth is, most people won't. In fact, co-workers tend to become what I call aiders and abettors, siding with the perpetrator instead of with you.

Anger, expressed in short-temperedness, being on edge all the time, exploding at the slightest provocation, is Stage Four. As harassment continues, you become angry. Seeing no way out of the situation leads to feelings of helplessness: in this stage, it seems as if anything and everything can set you off. Situations you used to deal with calmly now cause uncontrollable explosions of rage. Some people suffer crying spells at work. Too much bottled-up anger can lead to an emotional breakdown.

Physical Effects

Next come the physical manifestations of being sexually harassed. Skeptics may think I am describing only what happened to me. But the truth is, I am describing what happens to *most* victims. I have seen it.

Nearly all the physical effects are stress-related, but that doesn't make them any less real.

Headaches become progressively more frequent; some victims start to have migraines. You may break out in hives or rashes. You may be more susceptible to colds. One man I know who was being sexually harassed caught a cold every four weeks, like clockwork. Some people suffer anxiety attacks and even pass out on occasion.

Others lose their hair—it just falls out in clumps, as mind did. Insomnia is common.

Many people suffer urinary-tract infections, chronic fatigue, nausea, gastrointestinal problems, eating disorders—some react by overeating and gaining weight; others find it impossible to keep weight on and start losing dangerous amounts. Ulcers are not unusual; nor are other painful stomach disorders.

On-the-job injuries may become frequent, even if you've never been hurt before. It's not just a coincidence. You *are* more distracted. Another all-too-real cause of job-related injury is retaliation. When spurned, the harasser may teach you a lesson by making you physically vulnerable to an accident. Unfortunately, this kind of vindictiveness occurs all the time.

Feeling trapped, vulnerable, and humiliated—in short, powerless—leaves the door open for depression to set in, and with it, all sorts of side effects. One woman I counseled became so depressed she wouldn't leave the house. She stopped cleaning, refused to talk to her friends, and couldn't make love with her husband. Menstrual cycles can stop completely; chest pains can simulate a heart attack. In my case, I lost my ability to drive a car! When you're that stressed, you don't really want to go anywhere and can't enjoy a social life. You feel you have no friends, no one you can confide in. As one woman tearfully told me, "Everything was gone. I felt like no one could help."

As you'll see in the following chapters, marriages and family life are always adversely affected. Thirty-five percent of victims' marriages end in divorce.

Much has been taken away from you, not the least of which is the ability to function competently. The peace, joy, and harmony you may once have felt at work has been replaced by a hostile, offensive, and intimidating environment. Friendships have evaporated. Potential enemies hover around every corner. Am I making it sound like you're at war? Guess what? You are.

The longer the harassment continues, the more susceptible you become to having a nervous breakdown and at worst, to contemplating suicide. All victims need therapy, but few feel they can afford it. Some eventually end up hospitalized, unable to function at all; 5 percent of victims require psychiatric hospitalization.

Financial Losses

For someone who has never been in this position, the obvious response should be to quit—just leave the job. But anyone who is not independently wealthy knows exactly why most victims don't. We need the job, depend on the money, and must earn a living. It's that basic.

As soon as you have used up your sick days and are taking time off without pay, your finances are affected. Too much time off without pay, and the bills go unpaid, including the medical bills you are sure to accrue as a victim of sexual harassment. In the most dire circumstances, such as mine, you may lose your job entirely because of too much time off—and get to the point where you can't pay the rent or mortgage. People I have counseled have become homeless when, due to the effects of sexual harassment, they couldn't pay the rent and were tossed out on the street.

That's when you may begin to consider desperate measures, the unthinkable. I remember once looking at the prostitutes on the street beat—there were times when the fact that they were making money looked good to me. Can you imagine how low I was, emotionally and financially, to be even thinking that way?

What about health benefits, you may ask. Won't my company's policy protect me from the worst consequences? The answer is probably not. Although you are more than entitled to health benefits and workmen's compensation, expect the company to fight you every step of the way. They will send you to *their* doctor, who will sign documents saying your illness was caused by a preexisting condition; they will hire lawyers to defend the company against any action you threaten. They will find any excuse to "prove" that your illness is not job-related. Although you may fight it, as I did, it could take *years* before you get the back pay you are owed. In the meantime, how will you live?

The cruel irony is that the dire consequences of sexual harassment occur whether you take any action or not! Even if you overcome the fear of complaining, of being labeled a troublemaker or an outcast, and *do* take the proper steps, it won't stop the effects from haunting you. It can't. By being sexually harassed, you *have* been violated.

And even if you do all the things you're supposed to, it will still get worse before it gets better. That's a fact.

But in raw terms, A recent survey done by *Working Woman* magazine found:

25 percent of sexual harassment victims were either fired or forced to quit their jobs

27 percent said their self-confidence was seriously undermined

12 percent reported impaired health

13 percent felt they'd been dealt long-term career damage

FOUR

Could It Happen to You?

Sexual harassment is prevalent in all professions and cuts blindly across race, gender, age, and economic lines. The following stories are true. Some have been highly publicized in the press; others are from ASH files, from people I have known personally and counseled. Their stories are not unique. *None* provoked the instances of harassment suffered. Only *some* were able to recover and go on to live productive lives. In certain instances, the cases are still pending; the wounds are still open.

I hope that by reading a wide range of cases, you will be better equipped to recognize and deal with sexual harassment, thereby minimizing its consequences should it happen to you. (To preserve their privacy, the victims' names have been changed.)

Cases From ASH Files

The Bus Driver

Tara, a single mother who made her living as a bus driver, was attractive, personable, and popular, a woman who could handle her bus, her routes, and passengers as well as any man at the company. When she first started, she was married and seemed to have no problems. When she and her husband separated, however, two things happened: 1) Her ex left her with nothing, and the job became her lifeblood, the only way she could support her young daughter and maintain her home. 2) The men at the job decided she was now fair game.

When her supervisors and certain coworkers began to solicit her for dates, she responded by ignoring them. Most stopped bothering her, but one particular supervisor and her own union representative both continued to press. She finally confronted them and flat out said no, she wasn't interested.

As of that day, everything changed for her at work. Tara began getting what bus drivers call scut assignments: routes through dangerous neighborhoods. Her shift was changed from mornings to afternoons—making it much harder for her to care for her child, who was too young to be left home alone after school.

One day, her union rep told her to report to her supervisor in the maintenance area. Although she was uncomfortable about it, she didn't want to disobey a request from a superior. The maintenance area was completely dark—and she found herself alone with the supervisor. Immediately, he pushed her down against a bench and tried to kiss her. She resisted; he stopped but warned her that if she reported him, no one would believe her. It was her word against his. (This is a phrase you will hear again and again.)

Although she realized her union rep was an abettor, she went to him because it was the proper procedure. As she suspected, he knew exactly what was going on. He told her straight out: either have sex with both of them, or "wind up getting hurt."

Tara wound up hurt: assigned to drive a bus with faulty brakes, she plowed into a light pole and other cars. (Amazingly, she was the only one hurt in the accident.) In constant pain, she now wears a brace from her neck to her waist.

Did Tara ever try to get help while all this was going on? She most certainly did, but to no avail. She approached several women's and victims' organizations—and even paid dues to get into some—but none offered her any substantive help.

By the time I met her, she had been told she could not file a lawsuit because the statute of limitations had run out in her state. I was able to help her in two ways. First, I introduced her to other victims, who understood her pain because they'd been there too. Second, I helped Tara find an attorney who *was* able to file a lawsuit after the statute of limitations suit had expired. She won a judgment against her company and now lives on disability. Not exactly a happy ending, but better than others.

A Woman on the Road Crew

Barbara worked on a road crew on the state parkway in New Jersey. Although the only woman on her crew, she performed the same hard manual labor as the men: drove a truck, put salt down, shoveled ditches.

Her competence counted for little, however, among her male co-workers. To them, she'd invaded the boy's club, and they harassed her almost from day one. At headquarters, they'd leave dildos, catsup-soaked sanitary napkins, and pictures of penises on her desk. They punched a peephole in the wall of her dressing area that Barbara plugged up several times.

The constant harassment led, typically, to illness and an on-the-job injury. Still, because she needed the job, Barbara returned. When they saw they couldn't break her with harassment, her coworkers tried to get her fired. They complained that she took too many sick days and was often injured. The company held a hearing to determine if there were grounds for termination.

At this point, I was called in as a consultant. After going over the evidence with Barbara and her union representative, I discovered several interesting facts. She'd performed well on the job and did everything that was asked of her. Furthermore, Barbara took off *fewer* sick days than her male counterparts, and was injured less often than many of the men. Most incredible, no one, not even Barbara, realized this was a clear-cut case of sexual harassment. I sat them all down and explained the situation.

Once they understood, no one wanted to continue with the hearing or deal with a costly lawsuit. Instead, they all sat down for training sessions on sexual harassment, and guidelines were developed for the company; even better, the guidelines were enforced.

This story has a happy ending. Barbara kept her job, and the harassment stopped.

The Corrections Officer

Patricia worked at a juvenile correctional facility. She had a bubbly personality, was attractive, and looked quite a bit younger than her forty years. The work environment was clearly dangerous. The inmates, though under the age of eighteen, were all felons, imprisoned for murder, rape, robbery, drugs. Worse, from the start, Patricia recognized that some of her male coworkers were supplying the teenage offenders with drugs, alcohol, and even women for sexual purposes.

In spite of all the negatives, Patricia enjoyed her job and was good at it. She had no trouble adjusting to the environment, or the kids. But her male coworkers, supposedly professionals like her, made her life a living hell. When Patricia made it clear that she was not interested in anything beyond a professional relationship with any of them, she found herself in compromising situations and assigned to isolated areas with particularly rough kids. Still, she wasn't afraid. She could handle most of what came her way.

What broke Patricia was the night her male partner drugged her coffee and, she believes, took advantage of her sexually. In fact, Patricia feels that many of the male guards took advantage of her that night. When she confronted her partner about it the next night, he as much as admitted it by threatening her—he told her to say nothing to anyone "because we work in the kind of dangerous place where anything could happen to you." Patricia said nothing.

Devastated by the incident, she suddenly couldn't handle anything at work, eventually had a nervous breakdown, and ended up hospitalized.

When I met her, she was on disability. She came to ASH support group meetings for a year and, with our help, found an attorney. Ultimately, Patricia decided against filing a suit but instead put the harassment behind her, went back to school, and trained for another field. In other words, she decided to get on with her life and did.

The Police Officer

This story strikes particularly close to home, because it happened to a fellow police officer. Allison, like myself, had been planning on a career in law enforcement since high school. She loved being a cop and did her job so well that, in 1984, she was voted Greater Chamber of Commerce Police Officer of the Year.

The only thing Allison did not love about her job was the sexual harassment she faced every day.

One of her supervisors repeatedly told her how much he loved the springtime because he loved to watch women in revealing tops. An officer boasted to her that he was so sexually active he was sometimes debilitated; then, he asked Allison to have sex with him. Several co-workers flashed sexually explicit messages at her, and one kept a calendar on the wall with daily, erotic messages that he'd read aloud to her.

Allison spoke up, through the chain of command, just the way you're supposed to. But to no avail; the harassment continued. In fact, it got worse. She was denied a promotion, and later found out why: "The female officers who did get promoted were the ones who played along with the men's games. The ones who didn't, who simply did a good professional job on the force, got punished," she explained.

Allison suffered all the symptoms common to sexual harassment victims; eventually, she had a nervous breakdown and was hospitalized for three weeks. She returned to work and was put on light-duty assignment, but the work environment continued to be sexually offensive. She suffered a second breakdown.

Finally, she felt she had no choice but to go outside the department and file a sexual harassment suit. At this point her aim was to go on full medical disability. In direct response to her suit, Allison was ordered to undergo a departmental psychiatric exam. It didn't surprise *me* when they concluded her problems were "hereditary, and not job-related." A police department, like any other company, protects itself first and foremost. However, Allison's department findings were disputed by an independent medical evaluation that completely supported her claim.

Allison found a female attorney who told the court, "For the city and police department to push Allison from 'Officer of the Year' to a hospital bed... is not only illegal, it is outrageous. Her dedication to the job and good performance were not questioned. She was the type of officer that the city desperately needs."

The city settled out of court. Allison is now on permanent disability and will receive a total of $942,000, to be paid in $20,000

annual increments. Although she feels vindicated, she will never be a
police officer again—her dream was destroyed.

Sexual Harassment Happens to Men, Too

Roger is a male office worker. A gentle, kind, small-boned young
man who worked diligently for a large soft-drink company. Some
people find him effeminate, but Roger is straight. His supervisor,
who was gay, began coming on to him very overtly. He would kiss
Roger, grab his crotch and buttocks, and make jokes about having sex
with him. Roger immediately told the supervisor that he was straight
and in no way interested, which only prompted the supervisor to
continue.

When Roger talked to coworkers about the situation, they informed him that other men in his position had quit because of the
harassment—and further, that his supervisor's father held a very
powerful position at the company.

Nevertheless, Roger filed a formal complaint with the personnel
department and was fired.

He decided to sue the company for unlawful termination but found
few attorneys willing to buck such a prominent corporation. Eventually, he hired a lawyer and went on with the suit. He was offered a
settlement but refused it. Unfortunately, Roger lost his case due to a
loophole. Lawyers for the company found he'd falsified his résumé by
claiming to be a college graduate when, in fact, he was six credits
short.

Although devastated by the experience, Roger picked up the
pieces and moved on. After working with me at ASH, he went back to
school, completed college, and is now enrolled in law school. Roger's
is one of the success stories.

The Male Soldier

The military is one place where sexual harassment is very prevalent. For years, a sign in the Pentagon read: SEXUAL HARASSMENT IS
NOT FROWNED ON HERE, IT IS GRADED. That sign only recently came
down. Unfortunately, attitudes cannot be changed so easily. Additionally, the ban on homosexuals in the military leaves a wide-open
window for men to exploit women. "Sleep with me, or I'll spread the
word that you're a lesbian" has been used effectively in countless

cases. According to recent studies, three out of four women serving our country in all branches of the armed forces report being sexually harassed. This story, however, involves a married couple who were in the National Guard together, and it was the man who experienced the worst of it. *Christopher's* wife was actually his superior in rank, which seemed to make him a target.

During roll call each morning, Christopher was routinely asked if his wife performed oral sex and if she liked anal sex. When on maneuvers with his unit, he was threatened: "Whatever you get from her [sexually], we all are going to get." Although both he and his wife were upset, Christopher was more directly affected by the situation. When he tried to handle it on his own, he was reported for insubordination. His sense of powerlessness led to physical fights with other military personnel.

He complained to his EEOC officer but to no avail; the man happened to be a friend of one of the worst offenders. Counseling failed to address the problem completely. Christopher was eventually asked to leave the National Guard. He was offered an honorable discharge, but since he didn't want to leave under any circumstances, he ultimately received a dishonorable discharge.

Unfortunately, I didn't get a chance to work with Christopher until it was all over.

Women Harass Men, Too

While statistics show that more blacks than whites are sexually harassed, and more women than men, the reverse can be just as true and just as painful.

The Male Police Officer

Alex, a muscular and attractive white police officer, was recently divorced when his workplace harassment began. Alex's immediate superior was a black female sergeant, who was obviously attracted to him. She assigned him to be her corporal, or driver, which put them in close daily contact. One day after work she asked him to go out for a drink, and he accepted. They had consensual sex that night.

Immediately afterward, Alex knew he'd made a mistake and wanted to remedy it quickly. He told his sergeant he wanted a platonic relationship, that anything else might affect his job performance. The sergeant felt differently. She wanted the sexual relation-ship to continue and used her power as his supervisor to make sure they were together. She made up Alex's daily schedule so that he had to be with her often and she insisted he stay on as her driver, although he tried to get a transfer.

When she realized he was trying to get away from her, she became hostile. She left obscene messages in his locker and on his home answering machine. When those tactics didn't produce the desired result, the sergeant brought disciplinary action against Alex. That was when he realized she was threatening his livelihood.

As much as he wanted to report her, Alex felt the whole situation was partly his own fault for sleeping with her in the first place. Torn, he began to experience the stress-related illnesses that result from perpetual sexual harassment. That's when he found ASH.

I counseled Alex to take several steps. I told him first to confront her: to explain that even though she was attractive and he was flattered by the attention, he really did not want a sexual relation-ship. Further, he was terribly sorry if he'd led her to believe otherwise. I also advised him to start documenting each incident.

The next step was for Alex to report the entire experience to his union steward. This is one area where men—even those who have been victimized—have an advantage over women. Simply put, in my experience unions tend to be more supportive of men.

And that is how the situation was resolved. The union steward told the sergeant that if she continued to harass Alex, she was setting herself up for potential problems. With that *she* transferred to another department, and Alex was able to resume his career.

It Happens to Gays, Too

The Policewoman

Diane, a police officer in a small Southern town, was an attractive woman and good cop who also happened to be gay. When several coworkers and supervisors propositioned her, she made her sexual preference known and also informed them she was involved in a long-term, monogamous relationship. That's when the harassment esca-lated. Despite her exemplary performance on the force and superior showing on exams, she was denied promotions that were given to others on her shift who didn't do as well. When she questioned it, she was told by her supervisors to "sit down and think about it."

In addition, the officers began to leave obscene notes on her desk and anonymous messages on her phone machine. Dildos were left in her locker, and she was routinely called a dyke.

Finally, Diane was told straight out, "If you want to stay on here, you're going to have to sleep with one of us."

Complaining did Diane little good. When she followed the chain of command and took the proper steps, she was labeled a trouble-maker. Although the people she worked with knew her sexual preference, many of her small-town neighbors did not: the police department threatened her with exposure should she continue to file complaints.

Diane saw no way out of her situation except to start over in another field in another community. Harassment had effectively driven her out of town.

The Flight Attendant

Carol was a flight attendant with a major airline. In her case, it wasn't a stereotypical passenger who hassled her, but a male supervisor and some coworkers who not only made suggestive remarks, but also physically grabbed at her. When she could not stop them, she fell apart. When I met her, she was already physically devastated, and there wasn't much I could do to help her. She eventually relocated from her Atlanta home to New Jersey and is now still trying to pull her life back together.

At least one uplifting story about a flight attendant and sexual harassment offers a ray of hope for others in this position. On one flight, a male passenger was groping a flight attendant and refused to stop, even after other attendants and the copilot had spoken to him. The pilot made an unscheduled stop—the man was taken off the plane and charged with sexual harassment. This situation was handled immediately and correctly.

High-Profile Cases: Lawyers, Doctors, and Teachers

The previous stories are from ASH's files. The following experiences come from people, some of whom have climbed to the top of their professions, who have chosen to make their stories public. I cite them here to give you a wider view of the depth and breadth of the problem.

At a large international firm, a *woman lawyer* and her male colleagues were meeting around a conference table. When it was her turn to speak, she said, "I have two points. . . ," whereupon one of the other lawyers interrupted, "Yes you do, and they look wonderful." Everyone else laughed. The woman, of course, felt completely humiliated. The "joke" was her coworkers' way to avoid taking her seriously as a professional.

A *female doctor* was with a patient when a male physician walked in and said casually to her, "Hi, babe, just came to pick up a chart." By doing that, he instantly demoted the female physician in the eyes of her patient.

Probably the most well-known case of sexual harassment in the medical field is that of Dr. Frances Conley—one of the first female neurosurgeons in the country—who teaches at Stanford University School of Medicine in California. Tops in her field, well-respected and admired, Dr. Conley abruptly resigned her position in 1991 because of "a career-long pattern of sexual harassment" from colleagues and superiors. As Dr. Conley reported, she was often asked to go to bed by her male colleagues, "in jest, as a way to see if I could put up with the 'rules' of the men's club. It was not harmful physically, but mentally it was disgusting." She further told the press that if she disagreed with male colleagues, they said it was because she had premenstrual syndrome or was "on the rag."

When she talked to others about the harassment, she was always told, "Don't worry about it. That's the way men are. You don't make an issue out of it." At the time Dr. Conley took that advice. Later, she made her statement, loud and clear, by resigning and telling everyone why.

Dr. Conley eventually was persuaded to return to her position at Stanford and to work within the system for change. By helping to establish guidelines for her profession, Dr. Conley is doing exactly what I did: turning a bad situation into something positive.

Not everyone can do that.

Several *teachers*—women whose field is *not* male-dominated—have come forward to share their experiences. One teacher's principal continually grabbed at her and asked for pictures of herself in her underwear. Her first reaction—typically—was to ignore him and try to make a joke out of it. She didn't think he would really pursue it in a school setting, with other teachers and so many children around. But he did. When she refused to cooperate, he threatened to have her transferred or fired. Since she was untenured, she felt her entire future was at stake if she didn't cooperate with him; so she did. She felt cheapened, humiliated, and trapped. Eventually, she left the profession.

A *teacher's assistant* at a middle school was sexually harassed by a male colleague, who was "getting bolder every day." When she dared to make a formal complaint against him, she found herself a pariah at the school. As she tells it, "My name was suddenly 'That's the one.' I was pointed at, lied and joked about, and spent the rest of the term with no one saying more than three words to me. Most ignored me altogether. I was made to tell what happened to me in front of the school board *four times,* only to hear afterwards that 'We don't/can't believe this.' It didn't matter that I had witnesses, three of whom were students. I was denied a union representative. When I tried to bring in my own representative, I was told by the principal, 'This is school business, and the school will take care of it.' They did—I was fired the same day. I got a lawyer who couldn't have cared less. Going to the EEOC was a waste of time—they said there was a limit on the time I could file charges, and that it had passed. So a year has gone by and I wasted time depending on the wrong people. But it feels like it happened yesterday. I get so mad about it, especially when people on the school board tell me privately that this man has a history of being a sexual harasser.

"On my record, they tried to put that I was fired for misconduct. My husband says I should just let it go, but I keep thinking, what if he does this again? What if he does it to a twelve-year-old student who wouldn't know how to handle it?"

This woman's thinking is absolutely right. Most offenders repeat, and there's little doubt this one will find another victim soon. And maybe next time he won't pick on someone his own age.

It Happens Everywhere: From Washington to Hollywood

Is there any workplace exempt from sexual harassment? Not that I have found. As the Hill-Thomas hearings taught us so graphically, sexual harassment runs rampant in the halls of our own government agencies, even the one that exists to protect us from bias, the EEOC. As in other places, the struggle to be believed and taken seriously is an uphill battle. The motion picture, television, advertising, modeling, and recording industries may be the most rife with sexual harassment incidents because they are glamour fields, and in most cases, the product they sell *is* sex.

In a very powerful way, what we see on the screen shapes our own attitudes on male-female relationships. With "The Cosby Show" and "Roseanne," we've come a long way from the wiggle and jiggle of "Charlie's Angels," but by and large, movies and television shows glorify women not for their brains or professional capabilities—but for their sexy looks. On screens large and small, actresses dress provocatively and flirt outrageously to get what they want, on the job or at home.

Certainly in advertising, desirable women are used for one thing only—to sell a product. And ever since MTV, popular music has become increasingly visual: we don't just listen to the words anymore; scenes of sexy women being manipulated as men play out their adolescent fantasies on screen dominate. In rap music, especially, women are routinely trashed, referred to often in the most degrading terms. Music videos largely shape our children's views of society and the roles men and women play in it. They will take these attitudes with them into the work force.

Sexual exploitation on screen often leads to sexual harassment behind the scenes. The casting couch concept—that actresses have to sleep with producers and directors to get hired—is certainly nothing new. What *has* changed is that it is now illegal and more victims are going public. These next few cases have been given much play in the entertainment trade press.

Karen, a secretary who worked for a Hollywood mogul, was interviewed on a morning talk show about her own experience, which, she explained, started with incidental comments. Her boss would "joke," "I know you've slept with other married men—how about it with me?" Then it advanced to gestures: "He implied I was having oral sex with him by simulating it over the phone." Over her protests, it got worse. "He took me to lunch," she said, "and told me that if I wanted to get ahead, if I wanted to get a raise, I'd better sleep with him."

When she refused, he started a campaign of denigrating her work—berating her publicly. He even started proceedings to get her fired.

Karen challenged her boss by filing a complaint with his superiors and going up the chain of command. When that didn't work, she went outside the company, to her state's Department of Fair Employment and Housing. It was only after she threatened to take the case public that she was offered an out-of-court settlement in order to keep her quiet.

Although she was courageous and fought, Karen was demoted and is now out of the company altogether. She's taking the case to court, but even if she wins, she feels, "It's a black mark on my record."

Another high-profile Hollywood case involved a male boss and a male employee. Bill, an executive with a very successful independent motion picture company, filed sexual harassment charges against the president of the company, the founder, and the major studio associated with the company. In his complaint, Bill alleged that his boss "sexually harassed me in his private suite with verbal, sexual advances and requests for physical and sexual contact. [The boss] conditioned previous promises made regarding my promotion and salary advances." Bill refused the advances, which he felt were "offensive and hostile." Then, he was informed by several coworkers, either explicitly or implicitly, that if he did not go to his boss's hotel suite, there would be adverse consequences in terms of his promotion, salary increase, and writing deal.

When Bill reported the problems to the owner of the company, he was told to keep it quiet, not to go outside for advice or help. Disregarding that advice, he filed a complaint with his state fair employment agency. After he filed, attorneys for the company insisted an investigation *was* in progress, that the owner had acted properly within the confines of the law, but that it was one person's word against another. Bill's alleged harasser has completely denied all charges. Bill eventually lost his case.

Within the executive suite at a prestigious recording company, a secretary, Sue, filed a multimillion-dollar harassment suit against a general manager. Also named in the suit was the founder of the company and the Japanese-owned conglomerate that recently bought it.

According to the on-record complaint, Sue alleged that her boss repeatedly engaged in verbal and physical sexual assaults. He masturbated in front of her twice—and ordered her to clean up after him; He put his penis in her ear when she was on the phone; he exposed himself and ordered her to touch him; he continually grabbed her breasts and buttocks.

Her reaction—as she has written in her complaint, and is so typical in these cases—was severe emotional distress. She suffered internal injuries and began to fear for her physical well-being and even her life.

Sue stated that she complained to the human resources department and others in supervisory capacities, but in every case, she met with "hostile, malicious, and deliberately indifferent" reactions. No one wanted to deal with the situation because Sue's boss was a valued executive. Well-liked in the industry, he was known as a "rainmaker," bringing in business and making the company rich.

Eventually, Sue filed a lawsuit. Her boss has since left, but no one admits that her charges are the reason. "He's retired to pursue personal life," is the official company line. Since that time, she, too, is no longer at the company; she is still employed within the industry, but at a much smaller and less prestigious company. Sue's case is pending.

In another state the son of a fashion mogul was charged with sexually harassing *three* young models. "He sat down on the sofa next to me as close as he could and lay his arm around my neck and the other on my knee," said one model. "Then he tried to grab me. I told him to stop touching me." Although the man has denied the charges, his business partner has effectively barred him from entering the modeling agency he helped found. In papers filed, it was alleged that his behavior negatively affected business. The barred owner has countersued, claiming harassment never occurred and the models' complaints are a ploy to oust him. This case is pending.

There is strength in numbers—action is taken if there are complaints by more than one person. Justice can be served if more people recognize harassment when it takes place and stop tolerating it as "part of the game."

FIVE

The Ripple Effect: Coworkers, Friends, and Family Matters

What I've described so far is the devastating toll sexual harassment takes on the victim her/himself. What isn't as well publicized is the very real and just as powerful impact it has on everyone around the victim. She may be at the eye of the storm, but the rain and the thunder also crash down on those around her: coworkers, friends, and most especially, her family get drenched. As the victim, you may *feel* so all alone (and in many ways you are), but your situation absolutely affects every single person who comes into contact with you, especially those who love you.

Coworkers: Aiders and Abettors

It's easy to recognize the effect sexual harassment has on *co-workers*, for they are closest to the situation, confronted with it, possibly daily. Although most incidents of harassment are carried out in private, still there are times when a coworker will witness it. Perhaps she sees a surreptitious pat on a behind; or the manager's hand beneath the conference table, squeezing the knee of his assistant. As soon as the coworker realizes the overtures are not welcomed by the recipient, she has witnessed harassment. Maybe she overhears a couple of dirty jokes told to or about another worker, and maybe she is just as offended. A *Playboy* calendar on the supervisor's wall is bound to offend more than one person in an office. Or perhaps the victim has come out and tearfully confessed to a colleague that she is being harassed. Whatever the actual situation, the moment a coworker knows about it—one way or another—*her* workplace environment changes too. And until the harasser stops, or is stopped, things aren't going to be the same for her either.

When coworkers are aware of sexual harassment, I call them aiders and abettors. For no matter what the situation, coworkers have several reactions, and few of them support the victim. When it comes to sexual harassment, there is no middle ground: you're either with the victim or against her. Coworkers almost inevitably fall into line against her—by doing that, they aid and abet the harasser.

A coworker may start feeling guilty for not being supportive, for her strong instinct *not* to get involved. That's human nature. Or, she may be a devious type, who sees your harassment as a way to advance her own career. For as she bears witness, day after day, to another person being victimized, she will see that person's slow but sure downslide. And she just might see a place for herself up the ladder, as your foot slips off the rungs. What she won't see is the possibility that she herself could be the next victim.

The most common reaction by coworkers to sexual harassment, however, is resentment. For once it starts, they are forced to take sides, overtly or covertly. It's a no-win situation. Unfortunately, that anger is often misguided; many people still blame the victim instead of the harasser—"You must have done *something* to be singled out like this." The feeling that *you* have done something to disrupt the calm, to upset the applecart, is going to be widespread. That explanation is less threatening to their own careers. One coworker actually said to me, "You should have expected it. You're an attractive woman on the police force. You should have known what you were getting into. You overreacted and caused your own downfall."

Even if a coworker or friend *wants* to be supportive to the victim, most of the time she will decide against it. She may soul-search, or she may just go on instinct, but nine times out of ten, she will reach the same conclusion: if she sides with you, even by just being emotionally supportive and giving you a shoulder to cry on, she takes a big risk. Her own standing in the company could be affected, or worse, her own livelihood. By siding with the victim against a superior, a colleague could lose her job. That is the way she will perceive it, every time out. Trust me on that.

No matter how the cards play out in this rotten game of sexual harassment, working relationships inevitably change, and not for the better. The ability to work together, as part of a team, has been adversely affected. Aside from the seething resentment felt by both the victim and the coworker, you are very likely to fall apart at work so that others can no longer count on you to do your part. The others resent you further, and productivity is directly affected. How can you focus on a client's best interests when you're always looking over your shoulder? In some cases, like mine, when lives may be at stake, the ripple effect of sexual harassment can literally be deadly.

In my case, it was my own life out on a limb with an armed robber in a dark alley; but if a police officer (male or female) is being harassed and not concentrating on the job, John Q. Public may get hurt, too. When your accountant is being harassed, he may accidently confuse the numbers on your tax return. When the surgeon is being sexually harassed, would you want to be the patient lying on the operating table? I keep saying that sexual harassment affects *everybody*—are you starting to see why?

Friends Do Not Understand

Friends will understand all too clearly that sexual harassment has taken over your life, and they won't like it. Friends will not understand *why*—unless they have also been through it. They bear witness to your emotional downslide and are powerless to do anything about it. At first, they may feel helpless. And then they get angry—at you.

If you are being sexually harassed, you will quickly find out who your real friends are. Unfortunately, in most cases, you will find that you don't have many. Here's a hot flash: Most of your so-called friends won't be supportive. That will seem ironic, because on the surface it seems your friends have nothing to lose by lending support. It's not as if they are in the direct line of fire: they're not at your workplace; they are not affected financially.

But the truth is, when you are being sexually harassed, they've already lost something, and that is your friendship. You may not feel like seeing friends; you may disrupt weekly card games or shopping trips. You may be unavailable to chat on the phone the way you always used to. There are few ways that you can be the true, helpful friend you've always been if you are going through this personal crisis. Maybe you've become so shaken and absorbed in your problem that you've forgotten dates; maybe, like me, you are so severely affected, you've lost your ability to drive a car. And if a friend relies on you to carpool her child, her empathy will only go so far.

Certainly friends allow each other self-centered time-outs during crises, but if your situation is typical, it won't be short-lived. And after a while, even the closest of confidantes get fed up and start to look elsewhere for companionship.

Simply stated, when you are a victim of sexual harassment, you will no longer "be there" for your friends—and they will resent that. They will see you as all wrapped up in your problems, as being selfish. They might even tell you you're boring (as someone did to me). In one form or another they will say, "This is all you talk about, all you think about—c'mon, girl, give it a rest already." What a so-called friend actually said to me was this: "Girl, you act as if the whole world had stopped." Well,— my whole world *had* stopped.

Families Get Torn Apart

Coworkers lose you as a member of the team; friends lose you as a friend. But no one loses you more than your own family. For within the walls of your home is where the cuts run deepest, the devastation is most profound, and tragically, the hardest to undo.

There is a fantasy that the family provides nourishment: warm, loving support that feeds the soul and allows you to go out and deal with the big, bad world. But that fantasy is shattered irretrievably when sexual harassment threatens you and your livelihood. In *most* cases, the victim's family is hit hardest, and on every level: emotionally, physically, and financially. Understanding is hard to come by, support crumbles, and families are often torn apart.

My own story, although extreme, is a case illustration. The reactions of my parents, siblings, and husband aren't that different from those of most affected families. The important thing to remember is that my husband and I are still married—we are happier than we have ever been—my kids are healthy, and for the most part, I have made my peace with the surviving members of my family. After what you are about to read, that may come as a shock, but I offer it up-front as a measure of hope for anyone going through this horrible experience. We came through hell and back, and so can you.

At the time, February 1983, I wrote in my diary:

Dear Mrs. God,
There are days I feel very guilty for what has happened to my family, because of my decision to fight the sexual harassment and animalistic behavior I have been subjected to. It would have been so easy for me to just become one of the guys and sleep with the commander. But I just couldn't bring myself to do it. I often wonder if I could have done something different to avoid the problems I find myself drowning in. I force myself to go to work every night—even though I never know if I'm going to come home alive—because we need the money.

My situation at home was this: Bennett was a medical resident and we had two babies. He was making peanuts ($18,000 a year); I was the primary support of the family. Naturally, we looked ahead to brighter days when Bennett completed his training and could command a better salary. It was a dream we both held onto dearly. From Bennett's perspective, when the harassment started and I reacted to it, I derailed the dream.

That is what *most* spouses feel. We struggled to get him through medical school, internship, and residency. We could finally see the light at the end of the tunnel. Then (in his view) I went and screwed up the whole thing. How could I do this to him? To us?

When I became a target of sexual harassment at the precinct I felt so guilty.

Truth is, in my case Bennett wasn't involved at first. I did tell him, and it's not that he didn't believe me, exactly. He just didn't want to deal with it. And he didn't, for as long as he could. He didn't encourage me to talk about it, let alone try to help me find a solution. He didn't let me vent. He most certainly didn't support my decision to fight. Bennett never understood the full scope of what I was going through until my case went to trial.

From the day the harassment began, the shocks reverberated

through my household and my job as a wife and mother. I had anxiety attacks, my hair fell out, my menstrual cycle was interrupted, I couldn't drive or take care of the kids some days.

Things got much worse after I was hospitalized, especially when my disability pay was denied. We couldn't make ends meet. Bennett had to take two jobs; he was under intense pressure to try and find a way to pay the bills. As I've said, there were periods when we couldn't afford to buy Christmas presents for our children, when we couldn't provide for them at all. Stress was at an all-time high, tempers were frayed—frequently to the breaking point.

The worst moments came during August 1983 while I was allowed home from the psychiatric hospital for weekend leave after my two-week evaluation period. Bennett was distant toward me. Finally he told me, "You fucked up your job." Well, when he said that, I went off the deep end. I came after him, and I wanted to kill him. He ran into the bathroom and locked the door, and I tried to bang it down with my hands. I banged until my hands were bloody; then I started kicking it until I'd made a hole in the door.

My rage was fed by so many things. It wasn't only that *I* was the *victim* here, but also, *he* was one reason I'd been targeted. According to my coworkers, a doctor's wife doesn't "need" a job. When my co-workers insulted Bennett, I stood up for him, I didn't let anyone say anything negative about him. And now Bennett was blaming *me!*

I was really violent and out of control. I wanted him to feel the pain and hurt I was feeling. I would have done him serious damage had I been able. Thank God I didn't. Once I got the bathroom door open, I reared into him like a wild animal. Bennett is not a violent man, and the only way he could control me was to sit on me and hold my hands. So there we were, me screaming at him and him sitting on me, pinning my arms to the ground.

Since it was summer, our front door and windows were open. Neighbors, hearing the screams and the scuffling, came running over to help Bennett restrain me. And wouldn't you know it, who should be driving by the house at that very moment? The police.

Traditionally, cops stick together—but not this time. After all, I was practically a "drummed out" cop at that point. Besides, Bennett was a man, as were the cops who were driving by. *They* stuck together. They never even talked to me, just asked Bennett what was going on. Then, they called the supervisor, and four more policemen came by. Bennett told them I was under psychiatric care, giving them all sorts of ammunition to use against me when my case came to trial. Despite my rage, I could clearly see what was going on. I knew the system—Bennett didn't. Smiling at Bennett, the cops took notes, happy to have "confirmation" that I was indeed crazy. They were trying to paint me as a maniac. (In fact, the police department used this incident to show that my breakdown was not job-related, but caused instead by marital problems! No consideration was given to the cause of those marital problems: on-the-*job* sexual harassment. As you know, it took years for me to win my case and get my back pay.)

The cops asked Bennett if he wanted to press charges against me. I could see him thinking about it; but when they started reading me my rights and drawing up a warrant for my arrest, Bennett suddenly realized the severity of it all and came to his senses. Then they turned to me and asked if *I* wanted to press charges against *him*.

But damage had been done. Bennett and I had wanted to kill each other. We even began to doubt our love for one another at this point. Further, not only did the whole neighborhood know about it, the police did too. Just before my case went to trial, I decided to leave my husband.

But I didn't leave, because Bennett, although he hadn't been there for me earlier, did show up at the trial. The rest of my family—my adopted father, my grandmother, my brother—didn't come, even though I asked them to. My mother-in-law explained that she couldn't, she had a hairdresser's appointment! During the six-week trial, many relatives didn't even call me. My mother helped by taking care of the kids; she began to understand the gravity of the situation when, three months before the trial began, my children began to receive death threats.

My lawyer had told Bennett to show up in the courtroom, and he did. On the second day of the trial, I broke down completely, weeping uncontrollably, unable to continue with my testimony. Retelling my story was too painful. That was when Bennett finally began to understand what I was going through.

For my part, I had to work through all the resentment I felt toward him. I kept thinking that I'd been there for him, supported him all through medical school. But when I needed him most, he wasn't there. Through therapy, we both finally came to understand that Bennett gave to me, to our relationship, all he was really capable of at the time. There has been a great deal of forgiveness on both our parts. After the trial, he understood my decision, my need to make ASH my life's work, and to turn this negative into a positive. He respects that decision and helps out as best he can. In fact, Bennett has become a real crusader against sexual harassment. Whenever he overhears a conversation about it that is inaccurate, he goes over to whoever's talking and sets people straight. This is what has enabled us to move ahead and to get on with our lives.

Up-front, I told you that my story was extreme, but it's far from unique. Just as I felt guilty about "bringing this on" my family, so do most others. We victims feel we should be able to handle the situation at the workplace and not let it affect our home lives. Often, we don't ask for help from our parents, siblings, or our spouses.

Families almost never know what's going on, and they are almost never supportive when they find out.

A woman whose husband was being harassed at work told me that while it was going on, "I didn't have a husband for ten months. We had to separate." Another woman, herself a victim, wrote, "My family has not been sensitive. I was even cast out of an apartment I was sharing with my cousin. Because of sexual harassment, I was fired from my teaching job and working as a temp. My cousin said I wasn't making the money I *should* have been making—so he was throwing me out for not being able to pay my full share of the rent."

Family members commonly blame victims. They feel stressed, threatened financially, and don't know where to vent their frustrations; you are the nearest and most likely target. Even though it seems so unfair, they are not monsters. They are just human.

The ugly claws of sexual harassment reach out way past the workplace and into your home; they hold your entire family captive in their grip. How can you loosen that grip and save your family? The only one way I know is through therapy. I strongly advocate getting outside professional help for the entire family if you are in this situation. The entire family is being victimized, and the entire family will benefit from therapy.

I well understand that many people cannot afford a high-priced psychiatrist. In that case, go to a cleric for advice, or a mental-health clinic, or one of the many family-service organizations where payment is based on a sliding scale. It is important to hold the family together as a unit during this time of crisis. I cannot stress enough how important it is. Think of it this way: if your child was sick, you wouldn't hesitate to get help for him, no matter what the cost. Well, if you are the victim of sexual harassment, the whole family is sick—and needs attention immediately.

SIX

What You Should Do If You Are Being Sexually Harassed

As with any kind of abuse, the best scenario is to stop it before it goes too far. Barring that, fight it every step of the way. I call it *proactive, preventive* strategy. Here is a step-by-step, detailed, and effective list of do's and don'ts.

DO, first and foremost, recognize sexual harassment for what it is: *unwelcome* sexual advances, comments, or a hostile working environment. In some ways, this is the hardest thing to do. No one wants this to happen, but it *can* happen to anyone. We *all* start in denial, but we can't stay there.

DON'T assume that if you ignore it, it will go away. Not this one. The only time it "just goes away" is if it was never harassment to begin with, or if you take the necessary steps to nip it in the bud.

DO let the harasser know—immediately, the first time—that you don't like it. Ask him/her to please stop. This can be accomplished in several ways, depending on your situation. Some people can't express themselves verbally; saying "No" can be done very effectively *nonverbally,* by using body language. Simply, but deliberately, *move away* when someone comes too close. Sharply turn around, or shrug that hand off your shoulder. Shiver, to let someone know you're uncomfortable; freeze, if you were moving; stand up abruptly if you were sitting down. Don't laugh at risqué jokes; stare stonily ahead instead. Shift your focus away instead of maintaining eye contact.

If gestures don't work, you will have to be more straightforward. Tactfully but firmly, just say no. Don't smile, laugh, or act embarrassed. It isn't easy, but the longer you delay, the harder it will become. Remember, by definition, sexual harassment is *unwelcome* advances. It is your responsibility to make sure that the harasser understands that his/her actions are unwelcomed by you.

DON'T leave the door open—misinterpretation will fly right in. If you start out going along with a climate and attitudes that are offensive, it will be harder to make a convincing stand later on.

Example: just after being hired, in a desperate bid to fit in with her male coworkers, one woman laughed at and even participated in dirty-joke telling, even though some of it was directed at her. She felt offended and often humiliated, but went along with it all the same. Then, she decided to stop participating, hoping her coworkers would recognize this as a signal to stop as well. It did not. Instead, the jokes continued, and the situation escalated into an even more sexually hostile environment. After going to her supervisor and up the chain of command—all to no avail—the woman eventually filed a complaint with the EEOC. The EEOC rejected her claim for damages, concluding, "Simply ending her participation wasn't enough to put her employer on notice that the jokes and comments from coworkers were unwelcome." She should not, they said, have participated in the first place—and she *should* have let her employer know she was offended. Had she done that, they might have upheld her claim.

DO use prudent judgment in terms of professional behavior. If you act flirtatiously, you are sending the wrong message.

DON'T ask for or offer to do special favors for the harasser.

DON'T answer personal questions asked by the harasser.

DON'T fall into the talk-back trap. If someone attacks you verbally, don't get into a verbal volley on his level. That's exactly what he expects and wants! In other words, if he calls you a bitch, resist the temptation to say, "Look, dickhead, don't call me that." It's hard to claim foul language offends you if you use it too. It certainly leaves the door open to misinterpretation and weakens your argument in the end.

DO act responsibly and take responsibility for your actions. If you made a mistake and even unwittingly led someone on, say so. Own it, apologize, and state your position.

DON'T worry about the harasser's ego; consider your own self-respect first and foremost.

DON'T dress in a way that may invite comments of a sexual nature. Now I know I'm about to get a lot of flak for that one—because *nothing you wear gives anybody the right to sexually harass you.* No matter how short, how clingy, how low-cut an outfit is, there are never any circumstances in which, by mode of dress, you are "asking for it." But you, in fact, make it easier for some people to think otherwise. One writer drew this analogy: leaving your keys in the car doesn't give anyone the *right* to steal it, but you make it easier for a predisposed thief. And that's exactly the point. Sexual harassers look for victims. To his sick mind, you may be announcing yourself as next in line.

Another simple point: Certain styles of dress are more appropriate in the workplace than others. Dressing conservatively may not be your personal style, but it's a good idea. We all tend to judge each other by what we wear. Dressing provocatively leads people—not just harassers—to make certain assumptions about you. I do not say this is right, but it is real. Another reality is that many men, still back in the Stone Age, feel that a low-cut, tight sweater is an invitation to touch. You may think you're saying nothing by wearing a short skirt; a male coworker may think otherwise. Why put yourself in a poten-tially compromising position? Trust me on this one—it isn't worth it!

What if, on the other hand, you are in a work environment where sexy clothes are not only the norm, but required? Dress codes like that have actually been challenged in sexual harassment cases. In a Massachusetts lounge-restaurant, waitresses were *ordered* to wear very short hot pants. A day didn't go by without a waitress being subjected to degrading comments, hoots, whistles, and even pinch-ing and grabbing by the customers. The waitresses tried to get the dress code changed, but the owner wouldn't budge. Until they took him to court. Not only did they receive an out-of-court monetary award for damages, but the owner was forced to drop his degrading dress code requirement. Later, the EEOC ruled that "employers cannot require employees to wear sexually provocative and revealing outfits if such attire results in the employee being subjected to unwelcome sexual conduct." Those women won something not only for themselves, but also for many female employees who came after them.

Okay, let's say you've done all you could to prevent becoming a target of sexual harassment. You've encountered objectionable behavior, did nothing to encourage it and everything to discourage it, and still it continues. Here's the next level of step-by-step do's and don'ts.

DO talk about what is happening with someone you trust. I can't stress enough the need to discuss it first with someone who is *not* in the workplace with you. Family members may not be the right audience, as you saw in the last chapter. But you do need an outlet right from the start, a shoulder to cry on. Later on, you may need to prove that you told someone about it. Consider a close personal friend, a cleric, an acquaintance who's an attorney (you're not hiring anyone at this point, just talking). Best of all, if possible, talk to someone who's been through it. Who better to be supportive and to help than someone who knows the games and the pain? This is the time, in fact, to start seeking out support groups, like ASH. Refer to the Resource note at the end of this book.

DON'T, however, just complain about what is happening. Along with an explanation of events, tell a friend what steps you've already taken to resolve the situation. You may eventually need corroboration.

DO approach coworkers—gingerly!—but only to find out if anyone else has had a problem with your harasser. This is not the time to complain or accuse, just to nose around. Perhaps you will find someone who's also been suffering in silence—which will add much fuel to the fire when you do complain.

DON'T pour your heart out to coworkers about your situation, unless you are absolutely sure someone has been in the same position. As I detailed in the last chapter, in nearly every case I've seen, coworkers side with the harasser and become aiders and abettors to the harassment. Those people at work you thought were your friends will look out for number one first. The harasser is almost always in a powerful, supervisory position; coworkers—even the ones you have lunch with every day—want to keep their jobs more than they want to be your friend. They may simply be afraid of derailing their own career, of losing whatever footing they've gained within the company. As soon as you make your situation known, you will most likely be labeled a troublemaker, and people will be leery about siding with you. Conversely, some real back-stabbers lurk in every working environment, and they may see your situation as the perfect way to suck up to the supervisor and put their own careers on fast forward.

Other coworkers may simply be friends of the harasser. To them, he's a nice guy, and they don't want to see *him* attacked by you, even if he is guilty. In rare cases, some brave soul may stand up for you, but in general, don't expect support from others. In most cases, you are out there alone. I never said this was an easy place to be, but you must recognize it for what it is. Eventually, it paves the way for getting out and getting on with your life.

DO expect that many relationships with coworkers will be severed. If you felt merely uncomfortable before, as the harassment continues, you may start to feel isolated, alienated, and if things get worse, maybe even like a pariah.

DO begin to report the harassment formally. Follow the *chain of command*—whatever it is—in your workplace. Although this didn't work for me, it is still the proper strategy and *has* worked for many others. After trying to halt the harasser yourself, go to his/her immediate supervisor. If you don't let management know there's a problem, you effectively don't *have* a problem. So report the incident(s), as well as the steps you took to resolve it. You may be lucky; the supervisor may be able to cut it right off. You still get people who think you weren't *really* offended by those dirty jokes, that you really *do* want his arm around your waist, that you're just being coy when you say you don't. Going to his supervisor signals that you are serious—and that may be as far as the harassment goes.

You may not be so lucky, however. Many supervisors become aiders and abettors as well. Most, no matter how well-intentioned, just don't want to hear it and don't want to deal with it. Some will tell you to forget it, to brush it off, that you really don't want to make trouble. Some will side with the harasser, especially if he or she is a valuable employee who brings clients/money into the company.

Some supervisors *will* take action, but not necessarily the kind you want: they may transfer *you* to another department altogether. Worse still, some take your complaint as an invitation to do a little harassing of their own.

In any of those cases, of course, you go to the next level, perhaps the supervisor's manager, or the human resources department (it may be called Labor Relations or Personnel) if your company has one. Perhaps there's an affirmative action officer available for consultation. On that level, clearly ask that an official record be made of your complaint. You might also ask for an investigation.

DON'T be surprised if, even on this level, you still aren't taken seriously. In small companies, where there may be no sexual harassment policies—or if there are, no one's challenged them before—the tendency is still to try and ignore the problem.

DO go to your union steward or representative if you have one. As you've seen in the case histories I have shared, that sometimes solves the problem.

DO see if employee support groups are available.

DO keep documentation of the harassment. No matter how devastated or confused you may be, documentation is the most important weapon you may have to fight back with. In the absence of witnesses, your notes may be all you have, and they just may be enough. Get a small, spiral-bound notebook and write everything down: the name of the harasser, the day, the time, the circumstances, exactly what happened, and what you did about it, in as much detail as possible. Include direct quotes, names of witnesses, or patterns of harassment.

Here's a sample entry:

Tuesday, February 3, 1992, 1:30 P.M. I was at my desk, eating lunch. All the other secretaries went out to lunch, so I was in the room alone. Mr. Jones walked in and noticed immediately that we were alone. I asked him what he wanted, but he didn't answer. Instead, he walked behind me and grabbed my breasts, saying *that* was what he wanted. I told him to stop, pulled his hands off me, got up, and ran out of the office.

Another example:

Friday, June 17, 1992, 4:00 P.M. I was at my locker, collecting my belongings, about to leave for the day when Sergeant Smith came up and stood close to me, so close I felt uncomfortable. I moved away. He came closer again and said, "What are you doing later?" I told him I had plans and started to move away again. Then he said, "I've been watching you. I love the way your uniform clings to your tits, it's a real turn-on." I felt embarrassed and scared. He was leering at me. I tried to stay calm; I thanked him for the "compliment" and started to move on. Then, he put his arm around my waist and told me that maybe I should put my plans on hold for the night and come home with him. I told him that under no circumstances was I interested in dating him. Then he said, "I hear you're up for promotion—maybe you should rethink your plans for the evening." I was shaking. I was hoping I'd heard him wrong. But I didn't say anything; I was afraid. So I put him off and left.

Or, simply this:

On Wednesday and Friday of last week—May 5 and 7—Joe Grant and Louis Engel whistled at me and called me a whore. I told them to stop it and they didn't. They just laughed.

DON'T worry about not being a good writer; just put down plainly what happened. It might help to think of your documentation as a diary—like the one you might have kept in high school—or a journal. As I've said, sympathetic witnesses are rarely present. Documentation makes it more than just his word against yours. It may put you one step ahead of the game—you can be sure *he's* not keeping notes. He may, however, be keeping other kinds of notes: berating your work performance, especially if you have rebuffed his advances. That's exactly what happened in one case in which the EEOC decided against the victim. A female quality-engineering clerk said that her supervisor called her into his office, told her he'd been noticing her and liked the way she dressed. He said that he would like her "for himself," and if she cooperated, she would move up in the company. She spurned his advances, and he eventually told her that since she didn't want to play ball, he was just going to have to find her work not up to par and fire her. She went to the EEOC, which conducted an investigation. They concluded that since she had no witnesses (!) and no documentation, there was no evidence that her supervisor had ever subjected her to any sexual advances.

Further, her supervisor *had* kept (invented!) a well-documented record of her "poor work performance."

DO, if possible, make copies of your documentation.

DO, if possible, have your log witnessed periodically, by someone you've confided in and trust.

DO keep any letters, cards or notes—all of your documentation—in a secure place away from the office.

DO write a letter to your harasser. This strategy appeals to many who feel more comfortable writing than with direct physical confrontation. Other people, however, are too distressed to put anything coherent down on paper. I have found that letter writing can accomplish two crucial goals: it empowers you, because you feel that you are taking control of the situation, *doing* something about it. More important, it has been proven effective in getting the harasser to stop.

In a paper written for the *Harvard Business Review*, Professor Mary Rowe outlined exactly what such a letter should contain. It should include three sections. *In the first part*, state exactly what happened, in as much detail as possible. Example: "On March 30, 1992, I met you for a meeting about my work, and you said if I came to your house, my chances of advancement would be much better." Or, "At the office Christmas party, you pinched my behind and asked me to go to bed with you." *In the second part*, state your feelings about the incident(s): "When you did that, I felt humiliated and threatened." "When you said that, I got a knot in my stomach and felt nauseous." "Since you started pressuring me for dates, I can't sleep at night." "After you told me that I'd better sleep with you *or else*, I have been afraid for my life." *In the third part*, state clearly what you want: "I want you to stop bothering me." "I don't ever want you to touch me again or make remarks about my body." "I want our relationship to be purely professional from now on."

DO revise the letter several times before you send it. You want it to be clear and dispassionate, not hysterical rambling.

DO photocopy the letter and keep the copy in a safe place.

DO send it by registered or certified mail, or deliver it in person. If you deliver it by hand, take someone with you; don't go alone.

DON'T expect a reply, although you may ask for one.

DO expect results. Letters frighten harassers. He/she doesn't know who else has seen the letter or if you're using it in a formal complaint. Some harassers will be genuinely shocked that what they thought was friendly behavior was not viewed that way by you— there can be no excuse for "not knowing" now!

DO understand the other advantages of letter writing: when it works, it keeps the incident(s) quiet—you don't have to worry about being branded a troublemaker. You may not have to go to a superior or file a formal complaint or make charges in any way. And if it doesn't work, you've got your documentation *and* proof that you tried to do something about it.

DON'T be afraid to take a voice-activated microcassette recorder to work. It will feel strange and uncomfortable; the average person wouldn't normally think of it. After all, you have no training in espionage, which is what it feels like. Not everyone will be able to do this, but if you can, and find an inconspicuous place for it, you will have virtually incontestable evidence. Some manufacturers of pocketbook-size recorders are actually advertising them specifically as anti–sexual harassment tools. One firm, Spytech, urges: "Sexually harassed? Tape it, prove it, stop it, sue."

If the harassment continues, *DO* continue to collect evidence, while still going up the chain of command. Your next stop might be Internal Affairs, if such an organization exists in your workplace. For me, Internal Affairs was supposed to "police the police." It's the last step before taking your problem outside the company.

Complaints lodged with Internal Affairs are supposed to be kept confidential. Unfortunately, this is often not the case. Although it certainly wasn't in mine, I still advocate this as a necessary step, but you must understand the possible consequences as well.

Often, you must go outside the company. There's one more step before going to court, and with luck, it *could* end there. So, *DO* contact your State Division of Human Rights, or the Equal Employment Opportunity Commission (EEOC). Before explaining the procedure, I must caution you...

DON'T automatically assume you will get help there. In my experience, it's easy to get lost in the shuffle. The EEOC is a great concept, but like many government agencies, it is understaffed and overburdened with work. They are under pressure to resolve complaints quickly. They can't and don't do right by everyone who shows up with a legitimate complaint. For all sorts of reasons the EEOC may not be able to help you, but you *can* stack the deck in your favor by approaching them properly.

DO start by calling the main office; the toll-free number is 1-800-USA-EEOC (3362). Ask for the branch office closest to you.

DO know what the EEOC is empowered to do. They can: order an employer to end discriminatory practices (in your case, sexual harassment); order your reinstatement, hiring, reassignment, promotion, training, seniority rights, back pay, and other compensation and benefits. Sounds good so far, huh? But the EEOC *cannot* put your harasser behind bars or change the attitudes of the people you work with. The EEOC cannot force everyone to see that you were right, that their perception of you as a troublemaker is false. The EEOC cannot change human nature; only (some) human actions.

DO know that you are going to the EEOC to *file a claim.*

DO know that there is a statute of limitations on filing that claim— and it isn't very long. By law, you have 180 days from the last incident of sexual harassment to file. In many states, you may also file at the same time with a Fair Employment Practices Agency (often called the State Division of Human Rights). By doing that, you buy more time, between 240 and 300 days.

DO know that you can file in person, by mail, or by proxy (i.e., someone else may file on your behalf).

DON'T show up at EEOC offices in a state of hysteria, although that's exactly how you may feel by the time you get to this step. Victims who are hysterical, disorganized, or incoherent (and many are) are the most likely to fall through the cracks at the EEOC.

DO go *prepared.* Be ready to tell your story in calm, rational, chronological order. If you can't do that, go with a friend, someone who knows your story who *can* present it clearly. Take your evidence, whatever documentation you have, plus proof that you have gone through the in-house chain of command (government workers are *required* to do this before an EEOC counselor will even see them).

Your claim will then be investigated by an impartial EEOC counselor, someone assigned specifically to your case who will go into your workplace, assess the atmosphere, and solicit statements from your coworkers. It won't be pleasant. In fact, if you still work there, the investigation will have repercussions. Some of your colleagues, even those uninvolved in your suit, will be angry. Many will undoubtedly urge you to drop the claim. After filing a claim, many victims have even been fired.

In some cases, the EEOC will be able to resolve the problem— maybe to your liking, maybe not. If there is no resolution and the EEOC agrees that you have a very strong case, they will issue you a "right to sue" letter. In many states, you cannot pursue legal action without that letter. In very rare cases, the EEOC *chooses* to litigate a case and will represent you for free in court. But as I said, that's rare; don't even hope for it.

DO file criminal charges with the police if you have been assaulted, raped, or threatened with either.

DO expect several *months* to go by before you see any action at all. But believe me, you want to give them every opportunity to mediate and resolve the problem. Although in later chapters I give you all the information you need to go to court, I don't advocate litigation as anything but a last resort.

While all this is going on, I repeat: *DO* get all the emotional support you can. If you can't rely on family (and certainly not on co-workers), go to friends, your cleric, someone who's been through it. At the end of this book, I've listed some sources for outside support. Getting therapy is, as always, an excellent idea.

Last but not least, look inside *yourself* for support. One way is to stop thinking of yourself as a victim, which perpetuates the feeling of being weak and helpless. The Women's Legal Clinic in Los Angeles puts it this way: "You are not a victim. You are a human being, a working, contributing, valuable member of society who has *experienced* sexual harassment in the workplace."

SEVEN

But Why Didn't You *Do* Something?

The steps I just outlined are straightforward, logical, and simple enough to follow. Still, the reality is that most people don't.

Even after all the publicity and attendant awareness of the problem, *most* victims still do nothing. According to a recent *New York Times* poll, a minuscule *3 percent* of sexual harassment victims make a formal complaint, and those who do are in the most dire circumstances. The other 97 percent choose silence, opting to go along to get along. Why?

Attitudes: "If It Doesn't Bother Vanna..."

Before I go into the nuts-and-bolts reasons, I'd like to bring up something less obvious but very powerful. As much as celebrities like Gloria Steinem and Anita Hill take a public stand against sexual harassment, many other celebrities pooh-pooh it. *Those* stars are just as influential—perhaps more so—than the others who are declared feminists. For in our society, feminism is a much-maligned and misunderstood concept.

Vanna White, the hostess on the popular TV show *Wheel of Fortune*, is a celebrity sex symbol who may never have experienced real sexual harassment, but she spoke out about it. "Guys makes passes, blow whistles," she said, "I just throw it off my back. I don't think anything of it. That's the way it is. If someone raped me, that's a different story." That Ms. White feels sexual harassment would have to go as far as rape before it would bother her is tragic. It also speaks volumes of insensitivity toward everyday working women who aren't on TV and don't earn millions.

Helen Gurley Brown, the legendary editor of *Cosmopolitan* magazine who has influenced generations of women with her then radical ideas about sexual liberation, wrote an op-ed piece in the *Wall Street Journal*. She claimed to know all about what *isn't* sexual harassment and described a game she used to witness while working at an L.A. radio station years ago. It was called Scuttle and went like this: "All the (male) announcers and engineers would select a secretary, chase her through the halls... catch her, and take off her panties. The girl herself usually shrieked, screamed, flailed, blushed, threatened, and pretended to faint, but to my knowledge, no Scuttler was ever reported... au contraire, the girls wore their prettiest panties."

I find this not only nauseating, but incredibly insensitive. While a blind eye might have been turned toward this type of behavior years back, it is illegal today. My guess is that several of those secretaries were humiliated and enraged, but felt too powerless to do anything about it. And I'm terribly sad that now, too, in 1992, Ms. Brown finds this an appropriate way to describe her feelings on the issue. My interpretation of her remarks is that women don't have to be taken seriously when they say no. It's archaic attitudes like hers and Ms. White's that make our struggle for respect and equality that much harder.

"No One Will Believe Me Anyway"

From my own experience and working with other victims, I think I've heard just about every reason in the book for going along with harassment. They are all viable.

Many people remain silent for the simplest of reasons: *they still don't recognize it for what it is.* They feel uncomfortable, and maybe a part of them knows something's not kosher here, but they can't put a finger on the real problem. My hope, of course, is that after reading this book, ignorance will vanish as a valid reason for anyone. Many women and men understand what sexual harassment *is*, but aren't sure that what's happening to *them* is reason enough to speak up. Perhaps they share Vanna White's reasoning—as long as they're not physically hurt, they probably shouldn't bother.

Some people are just plain *embarrassed and ashamed*. After all, matters of a sexual nature are difficult for many even to think about, let alone discuss with someone else. Those from a strict religious background, or perhaps a culture where talking about sex is taboo, may simply be too embarrassed to speak out.

Fear is the major reason people don't report sexual harassment. It's the toughest one to overcome, for it paralyzes. Fear takes many forms: "I was afraid no one would believe me" is the most common one, reiterated by Anita Hill, who commented on TV's "60 Minutes," "Women are told, either by their harassers or others, that they *won't* be believed if they come forward."

"I'll Be Alienated From My Coworkers"

Another refrain heard time and again: "I was afraid that reporting it would lead to more trouble, and I didn't want to be labeled a troublemaker. All I ever wanted was to be thought of as a good soldier, so I never complained. I didn't want to be viewed as a problem."

Fear of being the subject of gossip, of office scuttlebutt, is another reason people think twice before speaking up. One woman put it this way: "I knew that once I walked into my supervisor's office to complain, the grapevine would be in full effect. People would soon start to stare when I walked by; fingers would be secretly pointed. I would be the main course at the lunchtime gossip mill, and I would be isolated, alienated. I didn't know if I could deal with that."

The fear of being judged adversely by coworkers is very real, especially if sexual harassment has been long tolerated at the workplace and others who have experienced it didn't speak up. Just because I was the first person in the Detroit police force to fight doesn't mean I was the first one harassed there. Many policewomen in my precinct were victimized, but they chose to stay and play the game. In situations like that, even when you know this is *not* okay, that you should not have to go along with it, when you look around and see that *everyone* else is going along with it, you start to think, What's wrong with me? How can all these other people possibly be wrong?

Well, maybe you're the only person with the guts to stand up to it. Remember, fear paralyzes most people. It is also possible that some coworkers don't experience what's going on as sexual harassment. Some may very well be back in the Dark Ages and actually welcome the remarks—which doesn't mean that you should.

Coworkers commonly feel you must have done something to cause the harassment—by flirting or dressing provocatively. Truth is, the concept of sexual harassment is at the same level of consciousness today as rape was fifteen years ago: the blame falls squarely on the victim. If Anita Hill's very public, very humiliating experience taught us anything, it's that accusers can quickly become the accused— which makes for double victimization.

Fear of retaliation by the harasser—and by his or her friends—is high on the hit parade of reasons victims stay silent. Even if the perpetrator cannot affect you professionally, thoughts always linger on other forms of personal retaliation.

Fear takes two distinct forms, depending on whether the victim is white collar or blue collar. White-collar workers are afraid of their career being derailed if they speak up; they risk their reputations. Blue-collar workers are terrified of losing their jobs altogether; they risk their financial lives. No one can say that one is worse than the other. Both can be devastating.

Professionals explain: "If I complain, there will be a black mark on my record." "I just know if I say something, they'll [management] deal with it by moving me to another department—in other words, I'll quietly be demoted." "I'll be squeezed out of all the good assignments." "It will cast a shadow over my entire career."

There are psychological reasons as well, more common among the professional set, for not wanting to speak up. Some victims actually fear *for* the harasser and worry that by pointing the finger, *he* will lose his job, perhaps even his marriage. Unless revenge is the primary motive for complaining, no one wants to feel responsible for such consequences. Putting the harasser's welfare above your own, however, is inappropriate in these circumstances.

Further, psychologists tell us that women often feel a responsibility to be the "emotional managers" of relationships. We feel the need to keep things friendly, that we should inherently be able to handle situations like these. Even if the reality of the situation tells us otherwise, that stumbling block effectively stops some people from taking action.

In the end, many feel that speaking up isn't worth it simply because "It will do more harm than good—and why would anyone want to commit professional suicide?"

The blue-collar worker experiences all those fears, plus this basic one: "If I speak up, one way or another, I will lose my job." Although studies show that 90 percent of sexual harassment victims *want* out of those jobs, they need that job and are terrified of being fired. Many, like myself, are the sole support of their families. Finding another job, especially after some seniority has been built up, is often especially difficult. The current economic climate in the United States only makes it that much more frightening to face the prospect of looking for another job.

Not having money to hire a lawyer is also something people consider when deciding whether or not to speak up, because of the possibility that their complaint must eventually be taken beyond the workplace. And legal battles often take years to wage—years possibly spent without income.

"Why Bother—It Won't Do Any Good Anyway"

Many victims sense that speaking up against harassment will be in vain. A 1992 *Working Woman* magazine survey found: Only 21 percent of victims who *did* speak up felt their complaints were dealt with justly. Over 60 percent said they were ignored, or that the offenders were given only token reprimands, a slap on the wrist. Worst of all, 25 percent of people who made an official complaint were fired or fored to quit.

I wish I could give logical and powerful comebacks to all these reasons—that in spite of them, sexual harassment shouldn't—mustn't—be tolerated in any situation. But I can't. The person citing the reasons finds them too painfully real, and nothing anyone can say will coax her/him out of silence.

Deciding what to do when faced with sexual harassment is a very personal matter. There is little encouragement out there in favor of speaking up. Dr. Frances Conley, the neurosurgeon at Stanford University who spoke out about her own experiences, warns, "Look before you make an issue of it. Do some risk-benefit analysis, because you *could* derail your career. Ask yourself, Is what I'm about to make an issue of important enough to risk ruining my career? Women still have to think carefully." *Time* magazine wrote: "Any decision about whether to take action or lodge a complaint is an economic one. If it might lead to the loss of a job, or alienation from co-workers, it may seem too costly, even for one's dignity or peace of mind."

There it is in a nutshell. Sexual harassment is a no-win situation. When you chose to remain silent, you feel cheapened and exploited; your self-esteem may be forever damaged. If you feel you *must* remain silent, you also feel trapped. Remember, most offenders will repeat, secure in the knowledge that they can harass others, because no one will ever step forward.

But if you make the decision to speak up, are you ready for the consequences? It's not a choice anyone wants to make; unfortunately, it's the reality for many of us.

False Accusations

Let's take a moment to turn the tables and look at the other side of the coin. False accusations of sexual harassment can and have been made.

The obvious question arises, Why would someone risk his/her own career and financial life for a lie? Not many people would, but there are a few.

One motive is revenge, especially in the case of a workplace affair gone sour. To the aggrieved party, leveling sexual harassment charges can look like the perfect retaliation. As one woman angrily told me, "He hurt me; now I want to hurt him just as bad. By charging sexual harassment, I can mess his life up real good." In some instances she can; in many others, of course, it can backfire.

Although this doesn't happen often, it *is* one of the reasons I counsel against interoffice dating.

Another oft-cited motive for bringing false charges is blackmail. This explanation is dredged up by the press nearly every time a famous or wealthy man is accused; it seems to cast women back in that old familiar negative role of "witch-manipulator." Whether the charges turn out to be true or false, doubt is planted in the collective public mind: Is she a gold digger, making this up just for the money? In most cases she is not, but in all fairness, we must acknowledge that on occasion, money is the actual motive.

The possibility of false accusations worries many men. Some companies take sexual harassment guidelines very seriously. One high-level manager at a large international bank says, "If someone comes to me with a charge, and I don't take *immediate* action, I could be fired." The attitude among men at his company, and several others, is that the deck is actually stacked in favor of the person bringing charges. "In my company, there is no requirement of proof," this manager says. "And in my department, many men feel very vulnerable. For example, even though I might say to a male, 'That's a nice suit, it looks good on you,' I've stopped saying anything remotely complimentary that is non-task-related to female employees. I just don't even want to take the chance of a casual comment being misconstrued."

In cases of false accusations that I am aware of, the emotional consequences have not been as severe as they are for harassment victims, but the tangible fallout can be destructive. Men (and women) have been transferred, demoted, and defamed before charges are proved false. Damage to one's character is more easily done than undone. Until the truth comes to light—and even sometimes after it does—there may always be questions in the minds of others. Alienation from coworkers is common. Marriages—perhaps not the strongest to begin with—have been destroyed due to false accusations.

If an employee is fired on that basis, he or she will find it hard to collect unemployment—and possibly harder still to find another job.

What should you do if you stand unjustly accused? You are entitled to the same rights and should take the same steps as any victim. First and foremost, the moment you are called in and informed that you have been accused, demand an investigation. At the same time, of course, strongly deny the charges. During the investigation, it's wise to keep your distance from the accuser (if you know who it is), and behave with utmost care around the office. If the investigation does not clear up the problem, take the next steps—same as any victim—

go right up the chain of command, to management, human resources, union representatives, the EEOC, taking it as far as you have to.

If falsely accused, you also have the right to sue. If you can prove that the charges were false and caused harm to your reputation and loss of your job, you may well collect damages. You may never undo the complete damage, but as I've said and continue to say, sexual harassment is always a no-win situation.

PART TWO

The Law and You

EIGHT

Deciding to Go to Court

The decision to take my case to court was the toughest of my life. But I had no other choice. I tried to resolve my problem by working my way up the chain of command, but that only made things worse. I knew I had to draw on the power of the law to make things better.

Hard Questions, Hard Choices

As a police officer, I had a lot of direct contact with the legal system. Even so, when I filed my suit, I wasn't prepared for the emotional, physical, and financial impact that ensued. I am writing this book in part to help you understand what's involved when you decide to prosecute such a case. As the saying goes, forewarned is forearmed. I also want to help you learn from my experience so you might avoid some of the mistakes I made. No one should have to go through what I did—self-inflicted injury, suicide attempt, psychiatric hospitalization—in the struggle to regain control of his or her life.

Before you call a lawyer, read all of these chapters on the process of going to court, what to expect during the trial, and what happens afterward in order to get the big picture.

Perhaps you are reading this chapter now because you feel you have done all you can and see no other option but to seek legal help.

For your own sake, stop right now and think a moment. Have you indeed exhausted all your options? Have you:

- told the person who harasses you in no uncertain terms to stop?
- talked to your supervisor (or to your supervisor's boss if necessary) about the problem?
- informed your union representative, if there is one, of the situation?
- complied with the steps of your company's sexual harassment policy, if any?
- spoken with coworkers?
- documented the harassment in any way—kept a journal of events, made copies of correspondence, etc.?
- taken part in therapy to help you understand what has happened to you and how to deal with it?

If the answer to all of the above is "Yes" and the harassment continues, then it's time for some deep soul-searching. Think carefully about the following questions. Talk them over with someone you trust.

If you go to court, do you hope to get:

- an apology from the perpetrator?
- your job back?
- a promotion you feel you were denied?
- an end to the threatening work environment?
- back pay?
- money to compensate your suffering?
- money to punish the wrongdoers?
- revenge?
- justice?

Every situation is different. Only you can decide what you need to feel good about yourself again and restore your sense of power over your life. Many victims simply want justice to be done. Often the only way this can be achieved is to ask for punitive damages to compensate for financial loss, destroyed reputation, physical and emotional distress, and loss of employability.

What resources can you bring to this fight? Are you able to withstand the emotional strain of a prolonged battle? My case was in the courts for three years; it took another five before I received my final payment. My marriage was strained almost to the breaking point. I became alienated from family and friends. Even if my husband hadn't received an appointment in a different city, I would have had to relocate anyway. Are you prepared to make this problem the focus of your life—and the life of your family—for an unknown number of years?

Can you rely on the support of other people? Do those who share your home understand your situation and know why you are taking this step? Are they willing to make the necessary sacrifices on your behalf? What are your friends' attitudes? Are you part of a support group that can offer guidance, insight, and the benefits of their own experience?

Are you prepared for the outcome, whatever it is? Although the situation is improving, not all sexual harassment cases are decided in favor of the victim. Many cases are settled out of court, without an admission of wrongdoing on the part of the accused. Would you accept such an outcome? If you lose—a very possible outcome—will you be able to return to the environment you found threatening, or are you able to make the necessary changes in your life to avoid that environment (change jobs, relocate, etc.)? Even if you win, your life will be changed forever. In my case, I could no longer be a police officer—the job I had dreamed of and had trained for.

These questions are posed not to discourage you from taking your case to court, but to awaken you to the reality of what lies ahead. The better prepared you are, the stronger you'll be; the stronger you are, the better your chances of winning. Your victory will be a victory for all victims in the fight to reclaim our dignity, our power, and our sense of self-worth.

Law: The Basics

This is a crash course in Law 101, your options in the legal system.

First, forget everything you've ever seen on television and in the movies. Shows like "Perry Mason" and "L.A. Law" simplify matters to the point of triviality. Most cases aren't filed, tried, and wrapped up neatly in sixty minutes (minus time for commercials). In fact, the vast majority take months, perhaps years, before they even come to trial. And few verdicts are ever final. Often the losing side appeals, hoping to reverse the verdict or lessen the punishment. The process drags on for what seems like forever.

So: forget fantasy, and get real.

Some Legal Terms You'll Need to Know

As the accuser filing a complaint, you are known as the *plaintiff.* The side defending itself against your charge is known as the *defendant.* Yours is the *prosecuting attorney,* the other side's is the *defense attorney.*

A sexual harassment case is usually a *civil matter.* In law, civil means that the case pertains to the rights of private individuals who are bringing action, whereas *criminal* cases are prosecuted by the government. In civil cases, most courts can impose penalties involving only monetary settlements. They can also order that certain actions be taken: community service, restoring a person's job, repaying back wages, giving promotions, and so on. What they *can't* do is impose punishments in the form of prison terms. (In a few states, for example Texas, sexual harassment can be considered a Class II misdemeanor—just below a felony. In such states a jail term can be imposed.) If, in the course of harassment, you were touched or assaulted and you want to charge the perpetrator with assault, then the case becomes a criminal matter. Criminal penalties involve time behind bars. Some harassment cases can be filed as both a civil and a criminal suit, if the behavior involved was criminal (e.g., indecent exposure, assault, or rape).

Your case will be tried in a court that has *jurisdiction* over the laws deemed to have been violated. If, for example, the federal civil rights law is at issue, then the case will be heard in a federal court. If a state law has been broken, a state court will be your legal route. It's unlikely that county or municipal courts will be involved, nor will small claims courts, where cases involving minor damages (usually under $1,000) are tried, often without the need for a professional lawyer.

Areas of Law

Sexual harassment charges can be filed under many different areas of law. Talk with your lawyer to see which gives you the best chance of winning.

Types of tort actions relevant to sexual harassment cases:
Assault and battery
Intentional infliction of emotional distress
Intentional interference with contractual relations
Invasion of privacy
Negligence in supervision
Wrongful discharge
Wrongful interference with business relations

For example, sexual harassment might be considered a violation of your basic human rights. In that instance, you would talk with your state or city human rights commission, whose job is to enforce local discrimination laws. These agencies try to bring the warring parties together to reach some kind of reconciliation. Each state is different; check with your local Civil Liberties Union for the laws in your area. Some states (not all) have the legal power to prosecute violations if they see cause to do so. At least eight states prohibit sexual harassment of workers: California, Connecticut, Illinois, Michigan, Minnesota, New York, North Dakota, and Wisconsin. Almost every other state has laws prohibiting sex discrimination against employees; these laws don't cover sexual harassment specifically, and so your case may be harder to prove.

Because victims of harassment often lose their jobs, cases are sometimes prosecuted under the area of unemployment law. The specific issue here is whether sexual harassment counts as a "good cause" for leaving a job voluntarily, thus entitling the victim to benefits. State laws vary widely in their definition of good cause.

Bringing a private suit is another possibility. This area of law is known as tort law. A tort is any wrongful act, damage, or injury done willfully, negligently, or because of some kind of liability. This is the same route you would take if, for example, you were injured in a fall on someone's property or because of a faulty product. In a sexual harassment tort action, the specific damage might be defined in a number of ways (see box).

A suit of this kind allows you to ask for punitive damages, plus damages for pain and suffering, in addition to actual damages (loss of income, for example), resulting from the wrongful act. Often tort settlements are for money only—they do not redress the problem in terms of hiring, seniority, or promotion. As a result they may bring personal satisfaction to the victim, but they do not go very far in correcting the problem of sexual harassment as a social-policy issue.

Tort law does not cover breach-of-contract cases. In one such case, a woman in New Hampshire was sexually harassed by her foreman. When she refused his advances, he placed her in a lower-paying job. A few weeks later she missed days of work while recovering from an operation. The foreman declared that she had quit voluntarily, and the company terminated her job. She sued for breach of contract. In this case, the woman might have set her sights too low. The jury found she was entitled to a small amount of compensation for actual damages. However, they refused to grant her damages for mental suffering, saying that such an award doesn't apply to a breach-of-contract case. Had she filed a tort action, she might have won a larger settlement.

Victims of sexual harassment have also successfully filed claims under the equal protection clause of the Fourteenth Amendment to the Constitution, the National Labor Relations Act (NLRA), the Racketeer Influenced and Corrupt Organizations Act, (RICO) and other similar laws.

Which brings us to another option: filing a suit through the Equal Employment Opportunity Commission (EEOC).

The EEOC

The EEOC grew out of the 1964 Civil Rights Act, a federal law. Title VII of that act prohibits employment discrimination on the basis of sex, as I described in chapter 2. As you know, I had no luck with the EEOC, but you may.

Under the EEOC provisions, people can sue if they were denied a job because they refused to submit to an employer's sexual demands, or if they submitted to the demands and were then hired.

Or, people can sue if they were denied promotion or a change to a better job because of their response to sexual demands.

Under the third provision, people can sue if sexually suggestive remarks, posters, behavior, and so on make it impossible for them to do their jobs properly. This is referred to as a "hostile work environment."

Suits filed under Title VII entitle victims to claim back wages—the sum they would have earned had they not been discriminated against. It also allows plaintiffs to sue for reinstatement—to be given their jobs back. They can also ask that the defendants pay their legal fees, which may be an important consideration.

For many years people filing charges with the EEOC could not have their cases heard before a jury, nor could they sue for punitive damages. However, the 1991 Civil Rights Act now grants harassment victims the right to a jury trial, and it also allows compensatory and punitive damages for financial and emotional harm; these awards are based on the size of the company. As I write this, the amount of such awards is limited to $300,000, but Congress is debating an amendment to lift that cap.

The person who sues through the EEOC need not be directly harassed. You may be the indirect victim of sexual discrimination if someone else submits to demands for sexual favors and is given the job or the promotion to which you were entitled.

One thing to keep in mind: Title VII handles only cases involving a company with fifteen or more employees. If your company is smaller than that, you must go through the state agency or pursue a private suit. The EEOC maintains a list of lawyers who handle Title VII cases.

The maze of federal bureaucracy may impede getting legal satisfaction through the EEOC. If you are not a federal employee, you have only 180 days (roughly six months) from the last violation to file a charge. If your state has a Fair Employment Practices Agency, you have 300 days. The EEOC is required to notify the people you name in the charge within ten days. However, before the EEOC investigates, it will turn the case over to the state or local Fair Employment Practices Agency, if there is one. The EEOC will wait up to four months before pursuing the case; the actual backlog, however, may be up to two or three years.

When you notify the EEOC of your complaint, you will need to go in person to speak with a caseworker. I suggest you bring someone with you when you go. This other person can help you in many ways: keeping you focused on your purpose, providing emotional and physical support, and serving as a witness to the meeting.

After its investigation, the EEOC may decide there is no reasonable cause to pursue a suit. If so, you may then demand that the EEOC review the case a second time. If this time your charge is upheld and evidence is found that sexual harassment did take place, the EEOC will first ask the local agency to try to arrange a settlement between the parties. If that fails, the case goes back to the commission to see if there are grounds for a possible lawsuit in the appropriate federal district court.

If the EEOC decides not to file a suit, it will issue a Notice of Right to Sue. With this document, plaintiffs can then proceed on their own to file a suit with a federal district court within 90 days.

Sometimes the EEOC, on its own initiative, may decide to bring a case to court if it feels the public interest would be served. That might happen in a case where an important precedent would be set or where a decision would have a nationwide impact.

If the EEOC decides to try a case, it will pay your defense costs. Sometimes, if the case involves a state or local government or a governmental agency, the EEOC may order a temporary action, such as giving the plaintiff his or her job back, until the final settlement is reached.

One drawback of this route is that not everyone lives near an EEOC office. If you live in a rural area, for example, you may have to travel to a large city, which might add time and expense to your already heavy burden. You can find out whether your area has a local EEOC field office by calling your library or looking in the phone book under the government listings. To speak with the EEOC directly, call 202-663-4900. Or you can call 1-800-669-4000, and your call will be automatically directed to the nearest field office. The agency publishes a booklet that answers many questions about its policies and procedures.

Other Avenues

I wish I could report that all special-interest groups are a valuable resource in helping people deal with sexual harassment cases. That, however, has not been my experience. Some of these groups have no particular legal clout nor any power to mediate or bring about any binding decisions. Another problem, in my view, is that some of these groups seem uninterested in helping you unless you are already a member. They are more interested in recruiting than in redressing wrongs.

Which Way to Go?

Through which of these avenues should you pursue your case? I can't tell you. Without knowing all the details of your situation, I wouldn't presume to make a recommendation; all I can do is present the options. I can tell you, however, there are no guarantees. My experience and instinct suggest that your chances are better on the state than the federal level. Jurors chosen from your state are more likely to be sensitive to your situation and more likely to relate to your experience. However, the dockets of federal courts tend to be less crowded than those of the state courts, so your case may take less time if you go the federal route.

The most important thing is for you to decide exactly what you want to get out of your suit. That choice will help you narrow down your options. Most harassment victims simply want to regain control of their lives. The courts cannot grant that. Judges and juries cannot reach into perpetrators' brains and turn a switch that changes their attitudes. But they can grant compensation in the form of money, or vindication in the form of promotion, and so on. Such judgments can help start the healing process.

Be sure you are clear about this. Ultimately, a harassment lawsuit is not about money. It is about a principle. Money is only a form of compensation that sends a clear message to perpetrators: you have done wrong, and you must suffer the consequences. A financial award is not an end unto itself but a tool for you to use in rebuilding your life.

Whom Do You Sue?

I sued the city of Detroit and the Detroit Police Department. I also sued the specific individuals involved. In filing claims, the rule of thumb is: sue everybody. Your target is not just the person(s) accused of doing the harassing. If the harassment took place on the job, then the targets of your suit are the perpetrator(s), the supervisor(s), and the company or agency itself.

There are two main reasons for that. First, it's much easier to drop a name from a suit than it is to add that name later.

Second, and more important, the courts have stated time and again that companies are legally responsible for the behavior of their employees—even if they are unaware of that behavior, and even if they have nonharassment policies in place. There are cases where people have complained about harassment, and the company took some halfhearted steps to correct it; later, during the trial, the company was found guilty of not acting quickly or firmly enough.

Keep in mind that when the harassment is committed by a co-worker other than a supervisor, employers are usually considered liable only if they had prior knowledge of the occurrence. You must also prove the employer had prior knowledge when the case involves a client or customer of the company. That's why it's crucial for you to notify your superiors immediately if someone harasses you—and to document that notification. If it happens again, you can then prove the company's prior knowledge.

Don't be afraid, then, to name your company in the suit. I've talked to many women who felt they didn't stand a chance against a huge corporation and its team of high-powered attorneys. Not so. If you have a strong case and a lot of guts—plus a good lawyer—you can prevail.

How Much Should You Ask for in Damages?

No one can put a price tag on your pain and suffering. Courts have awarded sexual harassment judgments as small as $1,500 and as large as several million dollars. Usually, if you win you will be awarded less than you ask; in some cases, though, juries have actually awarded more. If you win, however, especially if the amount involved is large, expect an appeal by the defendant—it's virtually automatic.

Most harassment victims simply want to get their lives back the way they were before. The reality is, that won't happen. When you've been emotionally devastated—and many people are—there is no returning to the status quo. You can't go home again.

In my suit I asked for $6.5 million in damages. I was eventually awarded $1.2 million. The amount was large enough to get my story on the national news. One unexpected benefit was that money talked: people were more willing to listen to me. They heard my story— good and loud.

Should You Have a Jury Trial?

The choice of having a jury decide your case is up to you. I believe there are *always* advantages to having a jury present. For one thing, juries tend to be much more sympathetic to victims than to defendants. A recent study showed that juries decide in favor of the plaintiff far more often than not. There are bound to be people on the jury who have gone through an experience similar to yours, or know someone who has. That sympathy may translate into higher awards for damages in civil suits. Make sure you tell your lawyer whether or not you want your case to be heard by a jury.

In most instances the jury will be composed of six—not twelve—people. The lawyers will interview each potential juror and may reject any individual *for cause*—meaning for some valid reason. They may also reject a certain number of them (three or four) for no stated cause at all. If you are a woman, your attorney may decide to reject some potential jurors because they are male, although that's not necessarily the best strategy. Some men *can* be as sensitive to your case as women—it depends on the individual.

One more point: you may indicate to your lawyer whether or not *you* want a certain individual to sit on the panel of jurors. Talk to the attorney before the jury-selection process begins about how to communicate your feelings appropriately. Whispering can be annoying, and the last thing you want to do is alienate the judge.

How Do You Prove Your Case?

One of the mixed blessings of our court system is that the accused person is innocent until proved guilty beyond a reasonable doubt. The burden of proof is on the accuser. Since most sexual harassment takes place outside the view of witnesses, the victim is at a disadvantage.

Talk to coworkers. It's likely that harassment is a pattern, and that you will turn up others who have been targets themselves. These individuals may be useful later as witnesses, should your case come to trial. As I've mentioned before, however, this is the exception rather than the rule, so don't count on them. Witnesses may "forget" what happened just before they are called to testify.

Your most solid proof is the records, correspondence, and journal documenting the harassment while it was occurring.

Will You Be Called to Testify?

Plan on taking the stand, the sooner the better. It's important that the jury see you, and see the impact of sexual harassment on a living, breathing human being. If the trial boils down to your word against the defendant's, you stand a better chance if you speak on your own behalf.

Will Your Dirty Linen Be Aired in Public?

For many women, the worst part of the trial is being forced to tell your story over and over to strangers, some of whom may not be sympathetic to your cause. There's no getting around it, that's a hard burden to bear. I can offer you hope that grew out of my own experience: the more you tell your story, the easier it gets. During a rare public appearance, Anita Hill stated that the most important thing we can do to end sexual harassment is to tell our stories—loud and clear. Each time you are forced to recount your experience, think of it as another nail in the coffin of sexual harassment.

The minute you file a charge against someone, the process called *disclosure* begins. Disclosure means that the defense can subpoena your medical, employment, and mental-health records. They can interview your friends and coworkers. Yes, they *are* trying to dig up dirt to use against you! Is this fair and legal? Unfortunately, yes. Is this painful and humiliating? You better believe it is.

However, there are some encouraging signs. In a recent case involving a woman who charged her former boss, a restaurant owner, with sexual harassment, the defense tried to get the court to compel her to reveal the names of everyone with whom she had had sexual relations for the past ten years. Their strategy was to prove that the woman was a slut and couldn't possibly have been harassed—they wanted to show that *she* had been the aggressor and was only filing suit because the restaurant owner had rejected her advances! The court ruled that past sexual behavior wouldn't prove whether that person would act the same way in the future. Instead, such questions would merely serve to "harass, intimidate, and discourage" the plaintiff from proceeding with her suit. The court was wise enough to see that if victims believed their sexual histories would be discussed as evidence, they would be reluctant to bring a case to trial.

Should You Settle Out of Court?

As my attorney and I approached the courtroom on the first day of our trial, the defense attorney stopped us and asked if $250,000 was the bottom-line settlement I would accept. My lawyer turned to me and said, "That's a lot of money." I responded, "Not enough to keep me from going to court. The bottom line for me is that I want the jury and the public to know what I've been through. I want my story to be heard." I would not be bought off. We pursued our case and, as you know, won damages exceeding $1 million.

Plaintiffs are often faced with an offer to settle out of court. Before the trial the judge will often order the two sides to discuss the problem, either through their lawyers or with a court-appointed mediator present. Your presence at such a meeting may or may not be required. The goal is to work out a deal that circumvents the costly and drawn-out procedure of hearing the case in court. Even if the suit *is* heard, either side may decide at any point to negotiate a settlement.

Whether you agree to settle is a matter between you and your conscience. Many alleged perpetrators are willing to settle, not because they feel guilty, but because they want the nuisance to go away—to buy you off with a fraction of the amount you were seeking. However, keep in mind that settling is not the same as an admission of guilt or a resolution. The question of whether your accusations were true or not will always linger without the jury to render its verdict. Worse, without pressure from the court, defendants may simply resume their practice of harassment, making life harder for the next unsuspecting victim who comes along.

For the victim, settling offers some advantages. It brings the painful trial process to an abrupt end. And it may bring you some money that you wouldn't have if you pursued the case and lost. You get immediate gratification, knowing that the other side caved in. You also get your money quicker. Even if you win a judgment, it may be years before you see the check. And you avoid the drawn-out appeal process that could reduce your payment or eliminate it entirely. Perhaps most important, a settlement allows you to get on with your life.

Lawyers say that, generally, when the mediators come back from talking to the defendants and offer a settlement larger than $50,000, it's a signal that you have a good case and the other side is afraid they might lose. That's not a fixed rule, but it is a way of sizing up your opponent's strategy—and a possible outcome.

How Will a Trial Affect Your Life?

They don't call it a *trial* for nothing. It is an ordeal in every sense of the word.

For one thing, the process takes an agonizingly long time. My case took six months just to put the complaint together! It was nearly three years after we filed the suit before it came before the judge. The trial itself can take weeks, sometimes months; the appeals can drag on for years after that.

Consider the impact on your immediate household during all of this. You may have lost your job or may be unable to work. Many victims of harassment develop ulcers, suffer breakdowns, or experience other severe medical problems. I am not the only victim to wind up in a hospital because of the stress and strain.

Without the income, your family's financial situation will get worse. If you are a single parent, you'll need a lot of help. Remember, too, that sometimes people who quit their jobs because of harassment are declared ineligible for unemployment benefits.

The trial will consume most of your mental and physical energy. You may be called to hearings, meetings with lawyers, and so on. You may thus be unavailable to your family—you can't drive the kids to soccer practice, or you'll have to miss your spouse's office party. Your marriage will be jeopardized.

Be prepared for some surprising responses from the people closest to you. Some members of my family were outraged that I would dare accuse police officers of such behavior! I know that behind my back some of my friends accused me of being lazy, saying I was hoping for a big settlement so I wouldn't have to work again. If that happens to you, I can only hope you find the strength to cut these people out of your life and get on with the job you know you have to do.

Another element to be aware of is the response of the public—people who know about you through the media. You may be buying a Coke in the 7-Eleven when someone comes up and begins talking to you about the case. Sometimes their remarks are less than friendly. You may be seen as a troublemaker, someone who's rocking the boat. You become a mirror of people's worst fears and impulses. There are times, too, when someone will offer you a kind word, a sympathetic glance, an encouraging touch. Those moments are priceless, and can be all you need to refuel your desire to continue your fight.

Again, I tell you these things not to frighten or deter you. My purpose instead is to empower you with the truth, so you can be ready for what lies ahead.

NINE

Finding the Right Lawyer

The first question many people ask when they consider filing a suit is "Do I really need a lawyer?" The answer, absolutely, is yes.

In this chapter I want to pass on what I've learned—from having been a police officer and a plaintiff in court, as well as from my experience working with dozens of harassment cases through ASH—about finding, hiring (and firing), and working with lawyers.

What Does a Lawyer Do?

Many people joke about lawyers as sharks or shysters. For one thing, if lawyers are any good, they can argue either side of a case with equal conviction, which creates the impression that they are uninterested in the truth, that they sometimes twist the truth. Also, if they do their job right, lawyers can be pretty persistent, filing an endless stream of motions, petitions, and statements. Sometimes it seems as if all these guys do is make work for themselves by dragging out the process so they can charge higher and higher fees.

I'm not going to say that all lawyers are models of professionalism and courtesy. There are bad lawyers, just as there are bad doctors, bad judges, bad clergy—and bad cops. But the majority are decent, honest men and women who provide the specialized skill and expertise you need if you want your story told before a jury—and certainly if you want a verdict in your favor.

Lawyers perform two key functions. First, they serve as your representative and spokesperson. When you file a suit, you are under enormous stress. Someone has done something wrong to you, and you want justice. Your emotions are high, and your judgment may be clouded. The lawyers' ability to see both sides of the case is an asset here. Before and during the trial, their objectivity makes it possible for them to negotiate calmly, to speak in your behalf formally and professionally, without losing their cool. They can phrase statements and demands in a noninflammatory way, which helps keep the lines of communication open. If you've tried to resolve your harassment claim face-to-face with the perpetrator or your employer, you know how hard *that* can be! In short, lawyers can reduce the emotional intensity of the process, which can be a real asset.

Second, lawyers guide you and your case through the legal bureaucracy. They know the correct procedures and understand the rules of the court—foreign territory to most of us. If you want to get out of a maze, find a guide who has been down that path before.

Some people see lawyers as nothing more than clever manipulators. The reality is that good attorneys are master strategists. They know a lot about human psychology and how the mind works. Because they anticipate many of the twists a case might take, they can cope with surprises.

During the trial, lawyers need to convey to the jury both the sequence and the emotional impact of events that they themselves did not witness. They must also explain and interpret circumstances so the judge and jury can see things from your point of view. If they do it right, the verdict will be in your favor.

How to Find a Lawyer

The easiest way to is to let your fingers do the walking. Look in the Yellow Pages under Lawyer Referral Services, organizations that keep lists of attorneys who practice various types of law. You want a lawyer who specializes in harassment. If the referral service doesn't list someone with that background, ask where else you might call. Don't bother calling your state civil rights division or the ACLU; neither makes referrals. If there is no referral service in your area, call your county bar association or Legal Aid Society. ASH also maintains a list of lawyers in certain parts of the country.

Know this, however, before you call: Referral services, even those sponsored by bar associations, charge a fee—thirty dollars, for example—for their help. Sometimes such a fee can be waived. You may also have to make an appointment to speak with an adviser in person. At first glance this may seem like a lot of trouble and expense just to get someone's phone number. There may be advantages to using a referral service, however. For one thing, it can quickly match your needs with the people who can best help you. And the fee you pay often entitles you to a consultation with the attorney. Talking with yet another stranger about your case may be difficult, but the more information you give, the easier it is to zero in on the right lawyer for you. In certain cases these organizations can help you negotiate a reduced fee with the attorney you select.

Another route that I've found very effective takes a little detective work on your part. Ask your librarian for help in tracking down newspaper articles about harassment cases tried in your city or state. Those articles will contain the names of the lawyers (or the firms) who handled the cases. Call them (if they won). If they are too far away from where you live, ask them to recommend someone in your area.

When meeting with an attorney, don't be intimidated. Remember, you are hiring, you are the customer, and you need to be pleased with what you're getting. Interview attorneys to find out about their experiences, attitudes, and approaches. If you find the person unsympathetic or uncaring, move on. You may be stuck with your choice for years—longer than some marriages last! Don't make hasty decisions.

Bring another person with you to the interview, someone you trust who has a strong presence, who is not afraid to ask questions, who can think clearly and logically, and who will look out for you. In these circumstances, two heads are definitely better than one. You are very vulnerable at this time. You are emotionally devastated and may not be thinking clearly. You absolutely must be comfortable with your legal representative if you want to succeed.

Don't give up. I spoke to many law firms before I hired an attorney. What I discovered is that many attorneys are reluctant to handle harassment cases because the risk of losing is high, the burden of proof is onerous, and the monetary judgments are often small. I rejected some lawyers, and some rejected me. Many refused to handle my case because it was too political—they didn't want to take on the entire city of Detroit, or they didn't want to alienate their buddies on the force. One turned me down because he was planning to go into politics himself and didn't want to be seen as opposing "law and order"! Some didn't think I had a case to begin with. That's why, if possible, it's important to come prepared with notes, documentation, lists of witnesses, and so on. You will need to show the lawyer you have grounds for a suit.

Another point: It may turn out that the people most willing to handle your case have little or no experience in this particular field of law. In fact, that's what happened to me. Ideally, though, law school prepares attorneys to handle many different cases, just as family doctors are trained to handle all types of illness.

Also, in dealing with sexual harassment, don't automatically assume that "the best man for a job is a woman." I did meet with some female attorneys, but our chemistry just wasn't right. However, I know of many other harassment cases where women lawyers performed brilliantly for their clients.

My advice: Go with your gut. Credentials are only one criterion. Someone who believes in you and your cause, who is willing to work for you and fight for you, is worth more than a stack of impressive-looking résumés. The man I finally selected had never actually argued a sexual harassment case before, but he seemed determined to give it his best shot. He was hungry; I was angry. Together we made a good team.

How Much Does a Lawyer Cost?

Lawyers are expensive. Some charge hundreds of dollars an hour. Your case can drag on for weeks or even years, and your final bill can be enormous. And, of course, the odds are that you're in a financial bind already. Many harassment victims quit or lose their jobs; some are denied unemployment. No one I know in these circumstances has money to burn.

At the very least, you are entitled to a free first consultation with a lawyer. More important, I strongly urge you to find a lawyer who will take your case on a *contingency basis. That means the lawyer only gets paid if and when you win, or if you settle the case out of court. If you lose, the lawyer is paid nothing.* Usually lawyers who agree to work on contingency ask for a certain percentage of the award—25 to 40, or even 50 percent. That may seem high, but remember, they're taking a chance that they won't be paid at all. Another advantage of this arrangement is that the lawyer's income is based on what you are awarded, not on the hourly charge. Say you win a settlement of $10,000. A contingency payment of one-third amounts to $3,333. However, if the lawyer worked on an hourly basis, his bill could easily be $10,000—or more. You'd be worse off than when you started.

The situation is slowly improving. More and more lawyers— especially women, especially those who identify themselves as feminists—are willing to accept these cases on a contingency basis.

An important point: Make your contingency deal with your lawyer at the beginning. Both of you should sign a legal document that clearly states the terms of your agreement. This document should also spell out what happens in case you or your lawyer decides to stop working together. Will you have to pay costs that have accrued to that point? And stay alert. I know of one case where a woman won a huge settlement, and suddenly the lawyer got a little greedy, deciding he was entitled to more than the one-third share they had agreed on; now he wanted half because he had been "so supportive."

Some lawyers have managed to pay themselves twice. If the court decides the defendant must pay the plaintiff's attorney's fees, an unscrupulous lawyer might deduct both the court-awarded attorneys' fees and also his percentage of the award fee and the contingency payment when the check arrives. Don't let this happen to you. Be aware and make sure you get a clear understanding of this with your lawyer and make sure it is included in the retainer's contract you sign with your attorney. The contingency payment is the fee.

Sometimes a lawyer will accept a case "pro bono" (meaning "for the good of the public"). If so, there will be no charge to you. This can happen in several ways. Many firms do pro bono work as a matter of policy. Or the state public defender's office may be so swamped that it orders all the law firms in the state to accept a certain number of pro bono cases. Yours may qualify. Sometimes a lawyer sees an oppor- tunity to make a name for himself or herself by taking on a precedent- setting case sure to garner enormous publicity. The lawyers in both the Baby M. surrogate-mother case and the Rodney King beating case in Los Angeles did their work for no pay. If your case involves unusual circumstances—if it raises a fundamental constitutional issue or would set a policy for a major industry—a lawyer may consider tackling it for free.

Big Firm? Little Firm?

In law, bigger is not always better. The high-power, many-partner law firms have some advantages. They have more support staff, known as paralegals, who can do some of the legwork and research necessary to support your case. They have more collective experience and knowledge, and their members can consult with each other on fine points of law. They also have higher overhead costs—more staff, more office space, more supplies and equipment—so their fees will likely be higher. I suspect, too, that these firms are less inclined to work on contingency. Big firms tend to represent high-paying corporate clients or class-action suits where a large number of plaintiffs file together.

A small firm or a lawyer with a solo practice may be able to give your case more close personal attention. Usually lawyers in small firms do their own research. Small firms have lower overhead and can charge less. They may be more willing to consider working on contingency. Their expertise may not be as broad, but that's not necessarily a big obstacle.

Keep Your Guard Up

Through ASH, I have heard of perhaps two dozen cases where women have been sexually harassed by the lawyers they hired.

For example, a woman I'll call Kim went through the nightmare of harassment on the job. She thought she saw daylight when she found a sympathetic attorney, a man who believed in her cause and agreed to be paid only if they won a judgment. He even helped her get workmen's compensation for an on-the-job injury. One day, during a consultation, he put the moves on her, trying to feel her breasts and jam his tongue in her ear. Horrified, Kim demanded that he stop. The lawyer then threatened that if she didn't "party" with him, she'd never get her compensation payments—at the time, her only source of income. Confused and frightened, Kim called ASH. She was terrified of the lawyer, but also afraid she'd never find another one who would help her. ASH was able to force the attorney to turn over Kim's files. Kim's life was already so complicated that she didn't want to file suit against him, but ASH filed complaints with his bar association.

As someone who has experienced sexual harassment, you are vulnerable. Sad to say, some people will continue to think of you as a victim, as someone whom they can hurt. I don't mean you should be paranoid and mistrustful of everyone you meet. I do mean, though, that you need to be especially wary during this time of recovery from your pain and humiliation.

It would be a good idea to bring someone with a clear head along with you to all of your meetings with your attorney.

You've Got a Lawyer—Now What?

Insist that your attorney explain in simple terms exactly what the legal process involves and what lies ahead. You need to be reassured, but you also need to know what to expect. Be aware that, generally, the whole process is designed to discourage people from pursuing their case; only the strongest will make it to the final rounds of the litigation tournament.

It's in your best interests to tell your lawyer everything that may have any bearing whatsoever on your case. If you are not completely open and aboveboard, a seemingly insignificant detail may derail your case. The truth is, once you file a lawsuit you may feel you no longer have a private life. Painful as it is, you must be ready to discuss past relationships, marital problems, family history of drug or alcohol problems—anything that could be seen as potentially damaging.

For example, remember Roger from chapter 4, who worked for a soft-drink manufacturer and lost his harassment case on the technical point that he'd lied on his job application? Had Roger mentioned this to his lawyer ahead of time, his side could have been ready for such a development and worked on strategies to keep their opponents from using it to such an advantage.

Your lawyer will instruct you about the process called *disclosure*. Once you file a claim, the other side has been put on notice that they must defend themselves against your charges. Often that means they will try to turn the tables on you and make it look like *you're* the one who should be on trial. For example, sometimes the defense claims that a sexual harassment victim "dressed provocatively" or "was asking for trouble" by her behavior. During disclosure, when each side investigates the other, the defense may try to dig up dirt from your past by talking to people who knew you, looking into your employment and medical records, and so on. It is not surprising that many harassment victims lose heart at this stage and withdraw their suits rather than face such scrutiny. All I can advise is to be strong and accept the fact that things get worse before they can get better.

At some point, before the case comes to trial, a judge may order both sides to attend a settlement hearing to work out some kind of agreement. The main purpose is to bring the two parties into face-to-face negotiations and possibly avoid a lengthy courtroom battle.

If no settlement is reached, you will be called on to make a *deposition.* Under oath, and in the presence of lawyers for both sides, the defendant(s), and a court stenographer, you will be questioned in detail about your claim. The transcript of this deposition is considered a sworn document, and you will be held accountable for its accuracy. Before the deposition your attorney should help you go over your story many times to make sure all the details are accurate, clear, and consistent. The defense will do their best to intimidate you. As you file your deposition you will be in the same room as your opponent. Your lawyer should help you use that fact to your advantage. Be as strong as you can be, and look the perpetrator in the eye as you tell of the pain and indignity that person inflicted on you. In a way, the deposition is a dress rehearsal for the even greater pressure of the trial to come.

Small-Town Matters

People in small towns face unique circumstances when it comes to getting legal help. A woman I'll call Linda was a cashier at a five-and-dime store in a rural western town. Her manager kept making suggestive remarks and pressuring her for a date. One night as she was closing out her cash register, he cornered her behind the counter and described his sexual fantasies to her. He kept asking, "Does that turn you on? Want to make my fantasy come true?" She managed to slip away from him, but the next day she was told she was fired because her cash drawer had been twenty dollars short the night before—which she knew wasn't true. Linda wanted to file charges, but there was only one lawyer in town, an old family friend. She was too embarrassed to deal with him. Besides, she didn't want everyone in town to know her business, knowing only too well the destructive power of small-town gossip and rumormongering. She couldn't bear to see her name plastered across the headlines of her local newspaper. She lost the will to fight and chose instead to relocate. "The thing that galls me most," she wrote in a letter to ASH, "was that I did nothing to stop that bastard manager, who's probably still hitting on every girl who takes the job."

If you live in a small town, or even in a close-knit community, you know the pressure that exists not to make waves or stir things up. I wish I could promise you that people will automatically rally to your side and support you. The truth is, all cases of sexual harassment change victims' lives radically, whether or not they decide to go to court. This is especially the case with people who don't have the shelter of anonymity that a large city can sometimes offer.

Get Involved—and Stay That Way

Just because you've retained an attorney doesn't mean your part in this drama is over. You need to stay actively involved. Doing so serves a threefold purpose: You educate yourself about the legal process. You keep an eye on the lawyer to make sure you're being properly represented. And you keep yourself busy, giving yourself something constructive to focus on.

Trust me, you'll need to stay focused so you can remain strong through the ordeal that is yet to come.

TEN

How to Prepare for the Courtroom Environment— Psychologically, Physically, Emotionally

It was the toughest week of my life. For six consecutive days I took the witness stand, telling my story of harassment before the judge, the jury, and a courtroom packed with spectators and reporters. The first day I cried endlessly as I relived those awful moments of pain and humiliation. As a cop I thought I was tough, but after being put through this wringer, I was emotionally and physically drained.

There was yet more to come. During the cross-examination the defense attorney grilled me on the most intimate details of my personal life. Oh, she had done her homework all right! She wanted to know about problems between me and my husband. She dredged up dirt about my family's troubles with drugs and alcohol. She read from the records of my time in the psychiatric institution. The low point came when, before the entire courtroom, she pressed for details about a gynecological problem I had experienced while hospitalized. I couldn't believe it! Of course, none of this had anything to do with my being sexually harassed. Nothing my lawyer did could have prepared me for that kind of ambush.

Fortunately, the defense attorney's tactics backfired. The jury was clearly angered by her abusive approach and sympathetic to my situation. My attorney landed counterpunches by underscoring the fact that I had had no psychiatric history *before* I had been harassed, that the abuse I experienced was what had put me in the hospital in the first place. He made it clear that I had distanced myself from my family's addictions. He showed how I had contributed to society by putting myself through school and becoming a cop. We won in the end, but it was an exhausting, nearly demoralizing battle.

After my experience in court, I formed ASH to share what I have learned, and to soften the impact of the legal process for others. I usually become involved in a case when the person claiming harassment has found an attorney and is preparing to go to court. I advise on everything from proper attire and manners to how to handle media coverage. I also try to help the lawyers, who sometimes lose sight of how the trial process affects their clients. This chapter covers what I've learned during countless hours spent in the courtroom as a consultant and an expert witness. Let's start with the basics.

What to Wear

Dress conservatively. A trial is no picnic; don't dress as if it were. Show respect to the judge on the bench by wearing dark colors and sensible styles. No jeans, T-shirts, or sneakers. Men should wear a jacket and tie, women, a skirt and blouse, dress, or other outfit appropriate in a business setting. Keep jewelry to a minimum—for women, simple earrings, unobtrusive necklace or brooch, no bracelets. If you're married, wear your ring. Your hair should be clean, cut, and combed.

Observe the Rules of Etiquette

A courtroom is like a church. Your lawyer should carefully coach you on the appropriate and inappropriate ways to behave in court. One important rule: Never speak with any member of the jury. During a trial, the jurors usually enter the courtroom through a separate entrance from the plaintiffs and the defendants. You're not even supposed to ride in the same elevator with them, because any contact between you and the jury may be grounds for a mistrial.

When a witness is on the stand, you may want to respond to what is being said. Don't. That's what I mean by maintaining control. Resist the urge, for example, to stand up and shout, "He's lying!" Don't whisper, groan, cluck your tongue, or otherwise show your reaction. Communicate only with your lawyer, and only by writing notes.

An anecdote from my trial illustrates the effectiveness of doing so. A female police sergeant, testifying that I had filed a number of personal-injury reports, tried to portray me as lazy, someone who wanted to go on disability to sponge off the city payroll. I knew the truth: that I was a hard-working cop on the beat who confronted life-threatening situations every day, while this witness—whose experience consisted of sitting behind a desk—had never faced anything more challenging than a stuck typewriter key. I passed a note to my attorney: "Ask her how much experience she has had patrolling the streets." He did. Her answer: None at all. Our side scored a telling point, that my injuries were battle scars, a sign of dedication to my job and not a sign of laziness.

You are required to be present for every trial session. You don't have the option of staying home just because you don't feel like atttending. If you are sick or have some other valid reason for staying away, the trial will recess until you are available again. Some trials continue every day, all day; others may have half-day or alternate-day sessions. It all depends on the judge's preferences and the courtroom schedule. If you have to travel any distance to the trial site, you must work out transportation and housing for the duration. It may be possible to network with people through various charitable organizations who can provide you with food and shelter during the course of the trial.

Take the Stand

Many times as a cop I stared down the barrel of a gun held by a frightened criminal. I ran into dark alleys and abandoned buildings, chasing desperate people who had nothing to lose. I saw firsthand the terrible impact of poverty and crime and violence on people's lives. Even so, taking the witness stand was among the most frightening and heart-wrenching moments of my life. Not even my mother's death a few years later was as hard to endure. There, in the tense atmosphere of the courtroom, under the gaze of dozens of people, having sworn an oath to tell the truth, I had to relive my story yet again. For strength I drew on three resources: my knowledge that what had happened to me was wrong; my faith that the truth would finally be heard; and prayer. And when the jury returned its verdict in my favor—a unanimous decision that the defendants were guilty— it was the most exhilarating, confirming moment of my life.

I can't lie to you. Testifying is tough. You will rehash your experience again and again, in graphic detail. You will sometimes have to answer complex questions with a simple yes or no. Every minor incident will be blown out of proportion. You will feel as if *you* are on trial, not the defendant. The defense attorney will dig up all the dirt from your past, will open every closet to search for skeletons. That's why, as I said earlier, it's essential that you be very open with your lawyer as you prepare your case for trial. In one case for which I served as consultant, the plaintiff was a young man harassed by his male boss. The defense grilled every one of the plaintiff's friends, going back to high school and the Boy Scouts, to discover whether he had ever had a homosexual encounter. In my case my marital problems, medical records, and family history were all entered as evidence. I felt as if I was living a headline right out of the *National Enquirer.*

One strategy you and your lawyer should consider is to take the high ground: testify first. I did, and I think it paid off. Recently, scientists who studied the trial process found that jury decisions are most influenced by the way the case is first presented. If you speak up early in the process, the jurors will tend to see all other evidence in light of your view of events, which can be a tremendous advantage.

If your lawyer has done the job properly, you will have been prepared to take the stand. You will have repeated your story often so that all the gaps are filled in and every detail is clear and consistent. Your lawyer will have played the role of defense attorney, so as to anticipate as many twists and turns as possible. You will have experienced the pressure of taking the stand, so that when the time comes you will know what to expect.

I tell you this to steel you for the hard reality. If you know how tough the process is, you can toughen yourself in preparation for it. At all times, keep your eye on the prize, which is to seek justice, put this event behind you, and get on with your life.

Look 'Em in the Eye

Eye contact is perhaps your greatest psychological weapon during the trial. The eyes, said a philosopher, are the windows of the soul. Look at the judge when he or she speaks to you. Look at the lawyers who question you. Look at the jury so they can relate to you more closely. And look at the perpetrator when you speak about what that person did to you. It's virtually impossible for someone who has committed a wrong to maintain eye contact with an accuser.

Be aware, too, that the jury will be watching you. Your facial expressions, your reactions may speak as loudly to them as all the evidence presented during the trial.

Maintain Control

Your hardest job will be to keep your cool under intense pressure. Remember, the defense attorney's job is to rattle you, to argue with you. You may be yelled at; you may be called names; you may feel humiliated. The other side will say some pretty nasty, even untrue, things about you. Don't rise to the bait, and don't sink to their level.

Like all performers, lawyers are aware of the power of effective timing. They will ask a series of questions, building detail upon detail, to prepare for a big payoff at the end—a question that explodes like a land mine. If you are aware of this strategy, you can turn it to your advantage by throwing off the timing. For example, rather than replying immediately, you could state that you didn't understand the question and ask that it be repeated or rephrased. If you manage this skillfully, you will disrupt the questioner's pace and defuse the impact of the interrogation. Sometimes attorneys get so frustrated, they begin yelling or they become abusive. When that happens, you win sympathy in the jury's eyes. At one point in my trial, for instance, the defense attorney screamed that I was lying and demanded that the judge hold me in contempt of court. She shouted that the trial was a circus, a mockery. Her voice was so loud that people from elsewhere in the building came to the courtroom to see what was going on. Her tactic backfired.

No matter how badly the defense attorney treats you, always be very respectful and polite. Kill the other side with kindness. The better you appear as a person, the worse the harassment—and your inquisition—will ultimately seem to the jury. At the start of each day during my trial, I made it a point to step to the defense table and say a few cheerful words of greeting to the attorney. That bothered her to no end. She simply could not look me in my eyes, and so she tried to avoid me. I believe that she realized I was a person, a fellow human being who had been hurt—and I think that took some of the wind out of her sails. Be careful, though, if the defense attorney is a male; the last thing you want to do is to give the appearance that you are flirting.

Let the Feelings Out

I just stressed the need to stay in control. Often, though, when you are recounting your harassment, you will become emotional. Tears will sting your eyes; your throat will tighten. That's okay. Many people think they should hold back their tears because crying is embarrassing or undignified. But how will the jury know the depth of your suffering unless you let them know? Don't misunderstand—I'm not saying you should fake tears. This is not a soap opera. Just respond honestly and openly to the feelings as they arise within you. Let the jury see and feel what you're going through.

Witnesses

In the pretrial period, while you are collecting documentation of your harassment, be aware that some of the people whose names appear in your records will be asked to appear as witnesses, either for you or against you. For this reason, do not discuss your documentation with coworkers unless it's absolutely necessary. And of course, the trial will change the nature of your relationship with these people. Don't be surprised if people you were once close to no longer want to associate with you once you file suit. Also, sometimes people who agree to testify on your behalf suddenly decide to back out when it comes time to take the oath. They may fear for their own jobs or safety if they speak out.

Call on Expert Witnesses

One way I help other victims of sexual harassment is by appearing in court to attest personally to the emotional and physical impact harassment can have. As an expert, I am often paid for my time. My opinion, however, is never for sale. I will not appear in cases where I do not believe that harassment exists, or if I sense that the purported victim is simply out to make a buck.

In the past five years I have testified in several dozen harassment trials and spent hundreds of hours counseling victims on their courtroom appearances. In one case I worked for a male client over a two-year period without receiving a dime. In another case involving two police officers in Philadelphia, I was in the courtroom every day for two weeks offering advice and support. I estimate that victims I have counseled have won judgments totaling over $3 million.

You and your lawyer should discuss the possibility of calling on an expert to testify on your behalf. Experts are useful in supplying objective data about harassment, educating the jury on aspects that neither you nor your attorney may be qualified to address. They can't prove that harassment took place in your case, but they lend weight and perspective to your arguments. Remember, though, that the other side is likely to bring in their *own* experts to try and discredit your evidence. In the final analysis, the best witness you have is yourself.

The Lie Detector

Many harassment victims wonder if they'll have to take a lie-detector test. Some volunteer to do so. However, such tests have been deemed unreliable as evidence. It's possible to administer the test or interpret the results in ways that affect the outcome, positively or negatively. In my contacts with hundreds of victims around the country, not once have I heard of a lie-detector test used as part of court proceedings.

Strength in Numbers

It's absolutely essential to have people on your side attend the trial as spectators. When you are on the witness stand, telling your story for the umpteenth time, you need to be able to look across the courtroom and see the faces of those who love you and understand what you are going through. It is your right to have people attend your trial. In some cases, though—for example, those with high exposure in the media—seats may be limited. If so, the court will hand out a certain number of tickets to the prosecution and to the defense.

Be sure the people whom you have asked to attend as spectators understand the need for propriety. Outbursts disrupt the proceedings, anger the judge, and may subject you to penalties for contempt of court. In one case in which I was involved, I could see the mother of the victim becoming upset by the terrible things beings said about her daughter. I led her out of the courtroom and calmed her down, reminding her that she needed to help her daughter by staying collected.

Dealing With the Media

During my trial, my name became a household word in Detroit. Every day news of the proceedings filled the tabloids and television screens. Part of the intense interest sprang from who I was: a black-Hispanic female police officer. Part arose from unique circumstances: I was taking on an entire city, and I was asking for a record-setting amount in damages.

How did I cope with all this exposure? As much as possible, I ignored it. I urge you to do the same. If your case has attracted media interest, don't read accounts of the trial; don't watch the news. The media are more interested in scandal and drama than in balanced, objective presentation of the facts. A newspaper account will condense six hours of testimony into a few paragraphs; a TV item will reduce it to a thirty-second recap. There is no way this kind of coverage can convey the reality of what you've been through. Don't frustrate yourself. Disregard it. Also, your attorney may advise you not to grant interviews or talk about your case with other people. Follow that advice.

If your trial attracts so much publicity that it becomes a circus, your lawyer can ask the judge to bar reporters from the courtroom. The right of freedom of speech, however, grants them the right to cover the trial from outside the courtroom.

Stay Focused

Remember the old story about the girl who carried a jug of milk to sell at the market? She got so caught up in her fantasy about how she was going to spend all the money that she dropped the jug and ended up with nothing. In one case I was involved with, two defendants were represented by the same attorney. During the trial, one defendant suddenly became obsessed with the thought that the other might end up with more money from the judgment (which they hadn't won yet, by the way). She hired her own attorney, disrupting the court proceedings and causing no end of confusion. The case was eventually decided in their favor, but the award was much lower than it might have been had the two codefendants stuck together. The lesson here is to stay focused on your goal.

Coping With Post-Traumatic Stress

As I will never tire of repeating, it's essential that you seek therapy as soon as you realize you are being or have been sexually harassed. The sooner you get help, the less the impact of post-traumatic stress will be. "Talking therapy" can help you address many of the underlying issues you face in dealing with harassment. Your doctor may also suggest short-term use of medications to relieve certain symptoms such as sleeplessness. During the second day of my trial, I became so overcome with anxiety that I collapsed. A doctor prescribed an anti-anxiety drug that calmed me down and enabled me to continue my fight. Remember that medications will not solve your problem. They can only help return you to your normal level of functioning.

Remember, too, that sexual harassment affects the entire family structure, not just the immediate victim. For that reason I strongly suggest family therapy, in which your partner, your children, and if necessary your parents, take part. During this ordeal you need to do all you can to preserve your support structure. Family therapy can help.

Doctors can keep your body strong, and therapists can help you think straight and stay on track emotionally. But you need to build up your spiritual strength as well. Talk to a member of the clergy, if you know one you trust. Many books of inspirational essays, poems, and meditations can speak to your heart. I found great solace in prayer. Perhaps you will too.

Coping With Financial Hardship

Even if you have somehow managed to hold on to your job or have found another job during this period, it may be virtually impossible for you to go to work while the trial is in process. If nothing else, you will have to attend all the court sessions. You need to conserve your energy for your legal battle. Take a leave of absence from work if necessary.

Clearly, the financial impact will be intense. You may be able to apply for workmen's compensation or unemployment. Be prepared, though, to have your company contest your application. It may be necessary for you to apply for welfare, food stamps, or other public assistance. Ask family members for help.

Take Care of Yourself

This is the most difficult and challenging time of your life. Eat nourishing, healthy foods. Exercise to stay in shape for your battle. Get lots of rest. Ultimately, you must take responsibility for your own well-being. Whatever the outcome of your case, treat yourself with the love and respect you deserve.

ELEVEN

The Aftermath of the Court Battle

My trial—and the record-setting damages I was awarded—made national headlines. For a few days after the verdict, I stayed in my house recovering from the ordeal. When I finally went out to buy groceries, strangers recognized me and stopped to chat. It was a little frightening; these people knew all about me, yet I didn't know them at all. Once it took me close to an hour to walk to a friend's house three doors away from my own because everyone on the street wanted to talk about the trial.

I didn't pursue my harassment case in court to become a celebrity, but to an extent that's what happened. All through the ordeal, I told myself I wouldn't change, I'd be the same old Cheri when it was over. I was kidding myself. Whether you win or lose your case, you can't go through a trial like that and not change. You wouldn't be human if that happened. In my case, I realized that if my victory was to mean anything, I had to do something to make a difference in the world. At that point I decided to dedicate my life to traveling around the country to raise awareness about sexual harassment.

Part of my work with ASH—and my purpose in this chapter—is to alert harassment victims to some of the difficulties they will face as they try to pick up the pieces of their shattered lives. Their trial in the courtroom may be over, but the trial of recovery from harassment continues.

Relationships

During the trial you'll learn who your real friends and family are. I found out the hard way. Many times I begged my relatives to attend courtroom sessions. I'm afraid, I said. I need you to be there for me. My grandfather came, of course. And my sister came. My mother couldn't, because she was looking after my kids.

But the rest of them wouldn't come. My brother never attended, even though I had saved his hide many times—someone had warned him to stay away from me because I was a troublemaker. My grandmother refused to come, saying: "This kind of trouble has happened to other women. What makes you so different, what makes you think you are better? Who do you think you are, to file a suit against the whole police department?" Another relative—the wife of a judge—told me I couldn't fight city hall, that I would never win. And, as mentioned earlier, my mother-in-law couldn't come because she had to get her hair done!

Believe it or not, something positive arose out of this. I realized who my real family was: my husband and my children. Despite the strain the lawsuit put on our marriage, Bennett was there for me in court. When the verdict was announced, it was his proud and smiling face I first looked on. We grew closer because of my ordeal. It took a lot of strength for me to cut loose from my family in Detroit, but I knew I had to move on with my life.

No one can predict what your situation will be, but I want to prepare you for the hard reality. You can't always count on other people to support you in your struggle. Sometimes friends and family desert you just when you need them most. Just be aware that as you change during this period, so will your relationships with other people. Once again, I strongly recommend that you seek therapy to help you manage the impact of these changes.

If You Win

In an ideal world, the jury would decide in your favor, the defendants would humbly apologize, you'd be handed a check for a huge amount, and the world would see you as a person who was wronged but who has been vindicated. Case closed.

Forget it. If you win, the other side will almost certainly appeal. To appeal, they must file a brief within a certain period of time, usually 30 to 90 days, which includes a complete transcript of the trial and specifies why the defense thinks the judgment was wrong. A panel of judges at the state appellate court will review this brief. Then one of several things happens. The appellate judges may uphold the finding of the lower court, and that will be the end of the matter. Or they may find that there *is* basis for a retrial, thus sending the case back to the lower court. Or they may agree to hear the case on appeal, or they may decide to accept all or part of the verdict but alter the amount to be paid.

If the defense loses the appeal, they may decide to pursue it further, through the state supreme court, the federal appeals court, and finally the United States Supreme Court. Eventually, though, they will exhaust their appeals and be compelled to accept the judgment. The whole process may take months, even years.

In my case, the defense did appeal. The conviction of three of the four defendants was thrown out, but the one against my commander was upheld; the amount of damages to be paid was also reduced somewhat. The defense appealed again, this time to the state supreme court, hoping to have the remaining conviction thrown out and the money award canceled, but the decision of the appellate court was upheld.

In some ways the appeal is less arduous than the initial trial. As plaintiff, you may never have to appear during the arguments. Or it may be necessary for you to come in and testify to clear up one or two points for the judge. Most of the business, however, can usually be transacted through your attorneys. This is important, because appellate courts are located in your state capital, which may be hundreds of miles from your home.

When you are awarded damages, the money is actually paid under the company's insurance policy. Naturally the insurer will do everything it can to avoid disbursing the sum, no matter what its size. Be prepared to wait for a long period, perhaps a year or more, before receiving the check. In my case, I didn't receive final payment until five years later.

If you are fortunate enough to win, consult a financial adviser. Any accumulated debts must be settled. Remember, too, that under the contingency arrangement your lawyer is entitled to part of the payment. You also need to manage any remaining money wisely. It's not likely you'll be able to retire immediately, but wise planning can relieve some of the financial pressure and allow you to make some major changes in your life.

Watch out for parasites. After I won my case, I was amazed at the requests for money I suddenly received. People I'd never met wrote asking me to give them money to build a house or buy a car. Every charity in the book (and some that weren't) solicited contributions. Many of my relatives—the same ones who refused to sit with me in the courtroom—were now hitting me up for a share of my award. Use your common sense and judgment. You owe nothing to anyone. Any money you are awarded is meant to compensate for your suffering. It is yours to use to rebuild your life.

If You Lose

You must be prepared to face the fact that your case may not prevail in a court of law. A verdict of not guilty may make you feel that you've wasted your time, that your struggle was for nothing. That isn't true. If nothing else, you fought to regain your dignity. You stood up to those who harmed you and confronted them eyeball-to-eyeball. You sent a signal to the world that harassment is wrong and that it must not be tolerated. That in itself is a victory.

Even if you lose, you have some options. For one thing, you, too, have the right to appeal the verdict. You and your lawyer should review the case carefully. It may be that new evidence in your favor—witnesses, documents, and so on—has come to light since the trial began. If such evidence is strong enough, use it as the basis for a retrial. A close reading of the transcript may reveal errors in the judicial process, such as an objection that was unfairly overruled. Another point to consider is whether you want to retain your lawyer or hire a new one. That, of course, depends on how effective you believe your attorney has been.

If your case was tried as a civil suit, it may be possible to file a criminal suit if criminal wrongdoing, such as assault or rape, was indeed involved.

Only you can decide if you want to pursue the matter further. Reexamine your motive for going to trial in the first place. If you wanted only to have your story heard by a jury of your peers, perhaps this is the end of the matter. If you will not be satisfied until the perpetrators have been declared guilty, you need to muster your courage and keep fighting. In some cases where the lawyer is not working on contingency, people pursue their cases because they want a cash award in order to pay off their huge legal fees.

They may still lose in the end, but they have the satisfaction—for what it's worth—of knowing they did everything they could possibly have done.

The Psychological Impact of Losing

If the verdict is not in your favor, you will doubtless experience a range of feelings: sadness, anger, frustration, denial, guilt, self-recrimination, self-doubt. The fact is, these are all emotions associated with grief. Grief is the normal response to loss, whether the death of a loved one or a dramatic change in one's circumstances. If you lose your case, give yourself time to grieve. You need to recover your sense of worth and your perspective. Therapy can help. So can taking part in a support group.

After his unsuccessful harassment trial, Roger—whom I've mentioned before—suffered a tremendous emotional setback. He had trouble accepting the fact that he had lost, and he desperately wanted to believe that what had happened wasn't his fault. He lost all sense of self-esteem. He was incapable of working. Some days he could barely drag himself out of bed.

One thing I did to help him snap out of his funk was to sit down with him while he wrote out some simple lists: things he liked about himself, things he disliked, his goals, things he might not have done correctly concerning the trial. We discussed each of these lists in great detail. In time he got a grip on the situation. He saw that, yes, perhaps he had acted in ways that contributed to his problem to some degree, and that he needed to accept responsibility for those actions. But in other areas he was truly a victim and was not to blame. He realized that what had happened was in the past and that he had no control over it nor power to change it. He saw, too, that his whole life

was ahead of him. He had his health, his brains, and his talent. It took
a year, but Roger finally got his act together.

One of the hardest things for people to deal with when they lose
their harassment cases in court is the feeling that no one believed
their story. Victims know what happened to them; they are the ones
who suffered the daily consequences of harassment. Yet they (and
their attorneys) were unable to convince the jury. Afterwards they
may begin to doubt everything about themselves. Their self-esteem
goes down the drain. Don't let that happen to you. Sit down, as Tim
did, and make a list of your strengths, your weaknesses, and your
goals. Be sure to include in the Strengths column the fact that you
had the guts to stand up to the person who harassed you and tell your
story in court.

Starting Over

After the trial you may find you want to—or have to—reinvent
your life from the ground up. Many harassment victims decide to
move to another city or state. No question, it's tough to pull yourself
up by the roots, especially when you have children and a spouse with
a career. But it may be tougher to stay where you are. You need to
discuss your options with your family openly and honestly. Again,
you will need professional counseling—single, group, marital, family—to get you through this time of transition. Many people find it
helpful to join (or start) a support group. You may want to offer your
services as a volunteer counselor, since those who have been down
this road are the ones best suited to helping others. Their knowledge
comes not from books, but from firsthand experience.

In my work with harassment victims, I've seen numerous cases
where people's lives improved dramatically when they started fresh.
They can put everything behind them and get on with their lives. They
go back to school and get that degree they've always wanted. They
find a new and better job; they make new and better friends.
Sometimes they move closer to relatives from whom they've been
estranged.

More than likely you will also change jobs. Having put your coworkers on trial, you probably won't return to the working environment that led to all this trouble. In my case, the verdict led me to my

new calling as someone devoted to helping other victims of harassment.

Role Model

During my trial a TV reporter handed me some letters that viewers had sent to me in care of her. I was surprised by their content. Most who wrote offered touching words of support and encouragement. They, too, had suffered harassment, and they saw me as a kind of champion, as someone who was fighting for the cause on their behalf. I drew tremendous strength from these letters. It was almost as if the reporter knew I needed an emotional boost at that very moment.

I pursued my case for my own satisfaction, not because I saw myself as any kind of role model. Nonetheless, that is what I have become. A similar thing happened to Anita Hill.

I'm not saying that a similar thing will happen to you, or that you need to become a public figure, or an advocate of human rights. One woman I counseled through ASH who won a cash settlement turned to me afterwards and said, "I can't be like you, Cheri. I just want to close this door and get on with my life. I don't want to feel that I'm obligated to help other people. It's hard enough just being who I am."

We each have our own calling. Simply be aware that other people will look on you as an example. And, of course, there will be those who resent you or who feel threatened by you. You have here an opportunity to grow into something larger than you might have ever thought possible.

PART THREE

Educating Management, Our Children, and Ourselves

Dealing with only the victims of sexual harassment is like putting a Band-Aid on a gunshot wound: it may stop the bleeding momentarily, but unless an operation is performed to remove the bullet and carefully clean and stitch up the wound, the patient will die anyway. This section is about removing the bullet and stitching up the wound; it's about getting to the root of sexual harassment, cleaning it out of our lives, and allowing a permanent healing to begin.

How do you tackle a problem so all-pervasive?

Education.

Companies, large and small, need to be educated about the necessity for sexual harassment guidelines, what they should be, and how to enforce them. They need to understand sexual harassment not as a woman's issue, but as a legal and business issue that affects productivity. *Our children* need to be educated—they need to know that you don't have to be grown up to be a harasser or a victim. They need to know that words hurt and can sometimes even be illegal. *We* need to be reeducated, in the way we think about each other, the way we talk to each other, the way we treat each other.

TWELVE

Education for Companies:
Dollars and Sense

Who's on the losing end of sexual harassment cases? *Everyone.*
Victims and their families, plus the harassers; that much is obvious.
But the biggest price, both literally and figuratively, is often paid by
the company that employs both the victim and the harasser. Here's a
first lesson for those employers and managers who didn't know: by
law, companies are responsible for the actions of their employees in
sexual harassment cases.

Here's how the Supreme Court worded it:

> An employer . . . is responsible for its acts and those of its agents
> and supervisory employees with respect to sexual harassment,
> regardless of whether the specific acts complained of were
> authorized or even forbidden by the employer, and *regardless of
> whether the employer knew or should have known* of their
> occurrence. . . . With respect to conduct between fellow em-
> ployees, an employer is responsible for acts of sexual harassment
> in the workplace where the employer (or its agents or super-
> visory employees) knows or should have known of the conduct,
> unless it can show that it took immediate and appropriate
> corrective action.

The Equal Employment Opportunity Commission says the same thing.

It no longer matters what you, as an employer, *think* about sexual harassment. Whether you deplore it, condone it, practice it yourself, or turn a blind eye when your employees harass others, you are now liable under the law. As a company owner or executive, and no matter what you thought about it before, your interest in the issue of sexual harassment must now be self-interest. For if it happens anywhere in your company and you don't take immediate action, *you are held responsible.* That means *your company* is liable to potential lawsuits, and *you personally* are as liable as the harassers themselves—you may not be covered by the company's insurance policy.

The Supreme Court's phrase "should have known" is what gets many employers in trouble. It means you must stay on top of what's going on in your organization. To keep informed, you must rely heavily on your supervisors—ironically, the very ones whom studies have shown to be *doing* much of the harassment. So you must look to several people, not just one.

Much is at stake here. An employer stands to lose not only valued employees, but valued executives. Bottom line: sexual harassment is illegal *and* expensive. You could be ordered to pay, and pay big. You leave yourself open to multimillion-dollar judgments. The cost of liability for sexual harassment is worth escaping.

The laws are not only on the books, but have been tested, time and again, in the courts. Here are some textbook examples, from the Bureau of Business Practices, in Waterford, Connecticut.

A Texas district court held that the employer failed to take prompt remedial action when a female quality-assurance inspector was subjected to verbal and physical sexual advances by her supervisor, despite her requests to him to stop and after she complained to her department head. The employer fired the harasser only after the victim's husband complained about sexually abusive calls made to his wife at home two months after the victim first complained to her department head. The court also held that the reason given for the victim's discharge (poor performance) was not legitimate, because her poor performance was caused by the harassment. *The plaintiff was awarded over two year's worth of back pay.*

In another case, a district court ordered an insurance company to pay a woman $1.3 million for lost wages *and* emotional distress, *plus* an additional $5 million in punitive damages.

In another instance, a restaurant owner was cited when an employee was harassed, not by another employee, but by a customer who touched a waitress and directed sexual jokes and comments at her. The waitress complained to the owner, who not only didn't reprimand the customer (who was a friend), but also fired the waitress when she filed a claim with the EEOC and spoke to a lawyer. The EEOC ruled that the owner had a duty to make it clear to his customers that sexual harassment of employees would not be tolerated. It further ruled that firing the waitress after her complaint and consultation with a lawyer was *unlawful retaliation*.

Another example: Female building attendants were required by their employer to wear provocative costumes. As a result, they were subjected to lewd comments from the general public. A district court held the employer responsible for making sexual harassment a condition of employment.

Yet another: A woman charged that her supervisor's sexual advances, comments, and other vulgarities created a demeaning work environment. Although a lower court dismissed the case—because the supervisor did not threaten her with loss of any job benefits—the appeals court reversed the ruling, saying that there was a tangible loss because a hostile work atmosphere has a negative effect on the "terms, conditions, or privileges of employment."

Should an employee go to court and win her or his case, the company is clearly liable to damages. However, your company can also lose big money before a verdict is ever delivered—in attorneys' fees as well as out-of-court settlements. A large percentage of sexual harassment cases get settled out of court—and don't think employers thus get off easier. One paid $7 million in such a settlement.

It is not enough merely to be aware of the law and have a company policy on sexual harassment in place. You need to see that your guidelines (whatever they are; see more about specific guidelines in the next chapter) are enforced.

Why? The personnel office of a large government agency regularly sent memos to all supervisors emphasizing the agency's policy against sexual harassment. The agency even sponsored seminars for its managers on how to recognize and deal with the problem. Despite its efforts, a female air-traffic controller sued the agency for harassment. The only woman in her crew, she told the court that she had endured months of vulgar, sexually offensive comments from her colleagues. She said that she finally complained to her supervisor when a co-worker continued to proposition her. The victim claimed that instead of reprimanding the worker, her supervisor suggested she submit to the man's advances to end the pestering. She then informed her boss's superior of the situation. He did nothing. Then another crew supervisor offered to transfer her to his group in exchange for sexual favors. At this point, the woman asserted, she decided to sue her employer. She felt the agency *had* to be aware of the harassment because it was so flagrant.

In court, the woman's supervisor admitted that her coworkers had called her obscene names, but he said his remark about submitting to her coworker's advances was just a joke. Other supervisors testified that sexual intimidation was a common complaint from female workers at the agency.

The agency maintained that it had a strictly enforced policy against sexual harassment. It emphasized its efforts to prevent the problem. It showed the court that it had spent time and money educating its supervisory personnel about sexual harassment in the workplace. In essence, the agency asserted that if any harassment occurred, it shouldn't be held liable because it had no knowledge of this particular incident.

Wrong, said the court. Not only did the obscene comments and behavior by the woman's fellow employees toward her create an "intimidating, hostile and offensive work environment," but the agency *should have been aware* of the problem, both because of its pervasive character and because of the woman's specific complaints to her superiors. The court said that the agency's policies—including its seminars—were not effective. It ordered the agency to reinstate the woman with back pay and pay her $50,000 for attorneys' fees. Lesson: issuing a strongly-worded official policy against sexual harassment is not enough. (According to a recent survey, a whopping 90 percent of Fortune 500 companies have received complaints of sexual harassment, even though three-quarters of these companies have policies in place.) You must make sure the policy is carried out on all levels of your organization. Seminars and memos are meaningless unless your managers are implementing the policy, not just giving it lip service.

Another Hot Flash for Employers Who Didn't Know

You lose big money because of sexual harassment, whether or not you ever talk to an attorney about it and whether or not the victim ever talks to an attorney.

According to a study printed in *USA Today* in 1991, government agencies alone lost more than *$267 million* in a two-year period because of absenteeism, job turnover, on-the-job injuries, and lost productivity—all directly related to sexual harassment. Among private-sector, Fortune 500 companies, the figure cited in surveys is *$6.7 million*—per company, per year—excluding the costs of responding to lawsuits. According to the financial publication *Treasury*, that figure will rise to over $1 billion to settle lawsuits over the next five years.

When sexual harassment is condoned in the workplace, morale is adversely affected, and thus productivity as well. Sexually harassed employees simply don't do their jobs very well: they lose their focus, and competence goes down the drain. No matter what kind of company you have, its success is based on the performance of its employees; when that performance level goes down, it takes the productivity of the company with it. *Your* company!

Sexually harassed employees are afraid to come to work. They call in sick. The longer the harassment goes on, the more chance an employee will in fact *be sick*, get injured, and need to go on disability. It happens all the time.

Whether or not an employee goes to court, there is sure to be gossip, innuendos, and perhaps even accusations among the staff. Not only is this distracting, it cannot fail to affect work. Office gossip, too, tends to wander beyond the perimeters of the workplace. Whether or not a specific case gets to court, other people *will* hear that sexual harassment is a problem in your company. The hint of bad publicity may turn talented people away from your company, or, worse, may steer potential clients in another direction (especially if your industry tends to be very conservative and image-conscious). Clearly, any sexual harassment cases that do make it to court also make it to the media, and this is not a situation where any publicity is good publicity. It has also been found that companies with high rates of sexual harassment also have high rates of racial harassment, discrimination, and other forms of unfair treatment. This is hardly the profile any organization wants.

In its definition of sexual harassment and the liabilities involved, the Supreme Court added a significant codicil:

> Prevention is the best tool for the elimination of sexual harassment. An employer should take all steps necessary to prevent sexual harassment from occurring, such as affirmatively raising the subject, expressing strong disapproval, developing appropriate sanctions, informing employees of their right to raise and how to raise the issue of harassment... and developing methods to sensitize all concerned.

THIRTEEN

Company Guidelines: What They Should Be and How to Enforce Them

The very best thing an employer can do about sexual harassment in the workplace is to prevent it from happening in the first place. I'm not suggesting that you can change the attitudes of the people who work for you, but you *can* change destructive behavior patterns. Make it clear to all employees that sexual harassment:

- is taken very seriously at your company
- creates an offensive and hostile work environment
- is a human rights issue *and* a productivity issue
- is intolerable under any circumstances
- will result in disciplinary action, including termination

Employees should also be made aware that anyone fired for proven sexual harassment is not eligible for unemployment compensation.

Let employees know that you welcome complaints from those who believe they have been harassed, and that you have a clear policy in effect. They must know that you will investigate each claim thoroughly; protect targets by permitting them to remain anonymous; and discipline offenders quickly and appropriately.

What Company Policy Should Be

An informal, verbal policy is no policy at all. All organizations, no matter what size, should have a clear, written sexual harassment policy. Further, the written policy should be updated and reissued once a year. From a purely practical viewpoint, written policies help strengthen the company's position if a legal suit is filed. A written policy offers clear guidance to supervisors who handle complaints, and it offers protection to managers who may otherwise become the "fall guy" when, down the road, others begin second-guessing how a complaint *should* have been handled. Most important of all, however, specific guidelines help all employees by defining offensive behavior—effectively removing the "I didn't realize this was harassment" excuse—and telling targets exactly what steps to take within the company.

I have also found that when a company does not develop a formal policy, supervisors often ignore or downplay complaints, increasing the chances that a suit will be filed. They also are likely to aggravate the problems with a "boys will be boys" attitude, and may even encourage or participate in sexual harassment incidents.

For all those reasons, I've found it helps to involve top and even mid-level management in formulating sexual harassment guidelines. Simply put, if they've had input in making the policy, they are much more likely to take it seriously and support it wholeheartedly.

What exactly should your policy statement contain? Although each company should customize policies to reflect the specific organization itself, still, the policy must spell out, in detail, procedures to be followed in case of a harassment complaint. In addition, the policy should state clearly how it will be enforced and what steps will be taken against anyone found guilty of harassment.

Company sexual harassment policies must include:

- The legal definition of sexual harassment (adapted from EEOC guidelines).
- A strong statement of employer disapproval, along with the assurance that the employer takes the issue very seriously and considers it a productivity issue.
- An exact description of prohibited behaviors. This may be the

most difficult item to draw up. It should be very specific and indigenous to your company. I suggest that female, minority, and gay executives be included on the team that creates and reviews the policy. Chapter 2 lists what constitutes harassment and can be used as a guideline.

- What steps the target of harassment should take. This should include suggestions on how to confront the harasser, how to inform the harasser clearly that his/her actions are unwelcome—and how to report them.
- List the names and phone extensions of several different people to go to with complaints. The usual procedure of starting with his/her supervisor may be uncomfortable for the target—especially since it's been shown time and time again that the supervisor *is* the harasser.
- How the complaint will be handled. Spell out that every complaint will be investigated and describe how that investigation will be conducted. It's important to indicate a timetable for the investigation of sexual harassment complaints, and make all employees aware of it.
- What disciplinary action the company will take when sexual harassment has been established.

Many companies opt for two sets of guidelines, one for general distribution and a more detailed statement of procedures for manager's handbooks. (These detailed procedures should include processes for judging and appealing harassment determinations.)

Whether or not you have included top and mid-level brass in the formulation of your harassment guidelines, ask selected employees to review it. They may catch gaffes such as unintentional double entendres. Such a review is yet another way of signaling your employees that this is a serious issue.

Once a policy is set, it should be distributed to all employees and managers as well as posted in all public areas. Further, I suggest that, if at all possible, managers call each employee into his/her office, hand-deliver a copy, and emphasize its importance at that moment. Handling it this way allows employees to ask questions they may be embarrassed to broach publicly. It also gives managers the chance to make sure the guidelines are fully understood by each employee.

If the policy is distributed through interoffice mail, then a department or company-wide discussion and education session should be arranged shortly thereafter.

In addition to annual updates, the policy should be given to all new employees, as well as to those newly appointed to managerial positions (to emphasize further that his/her new responsibilities include looking out for/handling instances of sexual harassment).

Now that you have some overall guidelines for developing policies, let's review an actual scenario and see how an investigation could be run.

What to Do When an Employee Comes to You With a Complaint

A young female employee comes into your office, visibly upset. She manages to tell you about a coworker who is relentlessly bothering her sexually, and who won't stop despite her requests. He thinks his behavior is funny. What's your reaction?

  a. You tell her to come back later; you'll talk about it with her when she's calmer.
  b. You think, That's not so bad; where's her sense of humor?
  c. You think, Maybe if I ignore this, it will go away.

The correct answer, of course, is None of the above. By now you know that as a supervisor, you are a legal agent of the company, and your actions can make the company liable. As a supervisor, your foremost responsibility—to protect yourself, your company, and all parties involved—is to take the complaint seriously.

When an employee comes to you with a complaint, don't downplay it, brush it off, or tell the employee, "We'll discuss this later—when you're not so emotional." Remember that for her to reveal the situation is probably an embarrassing, if not downright humiliating experience. It has probably taken your employee a great deal of fortitude to approach you, and she is well aware that by going to you, word may get out—and she is running the risk of hostile retaliation from the harasser and gossip from her coworkers.

Invite your employee to sit down and tell you the complete circumstances of the harassment. Try to make her feel at ease, and assure her that other than those who need to know—for example, the human resource director—everything she's about to tell you will be kept in complete confidence. Assure her that you take what she is saying seriously, and that you will be taking notes on the conversation to aid any formal or informal investigation.

Keep accurate notes and document all of your conversations—for the employee's sake as well as for your own and the company's. Should a legal suit be filed, you will need the notes to prove your vigilance in the matter. (Taping isn't necessary and is likely to make your employee uncomfortable.) During the conversation, ask for such details as:

- what exactly happened
- when it happened, and if there was more than one incident, their frequency
- whether there were any witnesses or any evidence
- how, if at all, the victim let the harasser know of her discomfort

Try to assess the seriousness of the incident, but keep your personal feelings and sympathies to yourself. You may feel the employee brought the situation on herself, that she's a chronic complainer, or even that you've done similar things and they're really no big deal. Whether your bias lies with the alleged harasser or with the victim, keep it to yourself and lead the conversation as professionally as possible.

During your discussion, also try to control your nonverbal body language. Avoid, for example, glancing nervously at your watch, jiggling change in your pocket, or reacting with facial expressions of disbelief, shock, or tension.

When the account is finished, simply thank the employee for coming to you with the information, and assure her that the situation will be looked into immediately. Don't otherwise offer your opinion on what *should* happen.

Promptly alert your own supervisor of the situation as well as the human resources and legal department of your company. As your investigation ensues, keep all informed of the progress—or, if there are people within your organization especially trained to deal with sexual harassment, turn the investigation over to one of them. In that case, your part in the process is over.

The Next Step

The next step, of course, is the investigation itself. Here's how it should play.

First, check the personnel file of the accused for any previous related incidents. Whether or not you find anything in the file, you will need to call the accused harasser in for an informal, confidential discussion. Often, the accused harasser holds a position senior to that of the target employee—and the tendency is to believe him over her. Whatever your belief, at this point keep it to yourself, and be as professional as possible. Simply let the person know that a complaint has been made. *Discuss the circumstance, but not the name of the person who complained.* Usually, the accused will ask, "Did Ann make the complaint?," naming the target. Don't fall into the trap of revealing the name. You promised the employee confidentiality, and that's a promise you must keep.

If you're lucky, the accused harasser won't need any chastising—perhaps it was a simple misunderstanding. The harasser may have been unaware of the effect of his behavior, and once informed of it, may feel genuine shame. If that's the case, once aired, it's over.

This, however, isn't the usual scenario. More commonly, both parties will present contradictory stories about the incident(s). The best strategy here is to give the accused offender a copy of the company's formal sexual harassment guidelines and go over them with him. While you are still protecting the name of the complainer, he may get the message loud and clear—and stop his offensive behavior. It is also crucial to inform him that a full investigation is under way, as required by company policy. If the harasser is truly innocent, he will welcome it. If not, the warning may be enough to get him to stop harassing.

Concurrently, you will need to question coworkers. Be as discreet as possible. Avoid naming names or referring to the specific circumstances. Instead, at this stage, ask your staff general questions: "Have you noticed or experienced any behavior that could be characterized as harassing?" may be sufficient. If there is harassment, it's common to find other targets among coworkers. Or, other colleagues may not have a complete picture but may be aware of helpful details. For example, they may have seen the alleged offender hanging around the woman's desk a lot, or calling her into his office—or they may have noticed that the target has seemed especially intimidated by this individual lately.

Conduct as thorough an investigation as possible. Talk to other supervisors and managers and as many employees as possible.

Whatever outcome is indicated, be sure that the complainant is informed first—not the alleged harasser. Discipline can range from warnings, reprimands, demotions, transfers, even terminations. Whatever action is taken should be applied consistently, and of course, conform to general company sexual harassment policies.

If You Suspect Harassment—But No One Has Come Forward

Even if no one has come forward complaining of sexual harassment, if you suspect it, as a manager it is your responsibility to take action. This is what the Supreme Court meant by "should have known." Approach the person you think is being harassed and talk with him/her—even if you feel very uncomfortable doing so. The kind of sudden behavior changes that signal sexual harassment might include:

- sudden absenteeism
- a sudden switch to a very conservative style of dressing
- a sudden withdrawal from social exchange
- clear discomfort around certain individuals
- office rumors
- vague inquiries about company harassment policies

Similarly, if you become aware that the complainant has become the target of retaliatory, vengeful actions, or damaging rumors, it's your duty to confront such behaviors.

What Your Work Environment Says

Policies are meaningless if they are undercut by a work environment that informally condones or even encourages unprofessional behavior such as sexual jokes, put-downs and innuendos, foul language, suggestive leering, aggressive partying, inappropriate photos and posters, and inappropriate behavior at conventions. Where these attitudes and behaviors are prevalent, sexual harassment is sure to follow. Supervisors and managers should look out for the kind of atmosphere they are fostering among subordinates. Are they actively discouraging this type of behavior, turning a blind eye to it, or encouraging it? If a supervisor is aware of such behavior and ignores it, it's likely to escalate into a much more troublesome—and recalcitrant—problem later.

A growing number of companies are prohibiting sexually loaded language and behavior in the workplace. The same thing goes for dating between coworkers (the reasoning, as we've discussed, is that if a relationship sours, the potential for harassment increases).

The Importance of Training

As crucial as it is to develop and enforce formal policies, without proper training—for both managers and workers—they may still be for naught. A half-day training session can make a big difference in raising awareness of the problem and eliminating it from the workplace. Several consulting firms, including my own, will come into your workplace to conduct training workshops.

ASH workshops, were developed in consultation with Mona Harris-Ross of Houston, Texas, a consultant and trainer with an MED (Masters in Education Assistant). The workshops focus on prevention and education. We emphasize a proactive response, encouraging our clients to take steps *before* sexual harassment becomes an issue.

To those who say, "We don't have sexual harassment in our organization," we say, "Don't bet on it." The mere fact that surveys consistently find a majority of women have experienced sexual harassment at work should be enough to encourage management to address the situation. Some top supervisors and managers balk at this, saying "If there's sexual harassment going on, I'd have heard about it." Not necessarily. Remember that harassing behavior often takes place in private, and the target and certainly the harasser are unlikely to come to you—until things get out of hand.

Our Workshops

When a company calls for a consult, I ask:

- the organization's size
- who the audience for the presentation will be (proportion of men

and women, staff and management, educational level of all participants, etc.)
- if complaints have been lodged, or related problems reported
- if the company has a sexual harassment policy (if so, I ask for a copy to evaluate it)
- if the organization has implemented training of any type on this subject, and for whom
- if the company wants to address any particular issues

Based on this preliminary information, Mona Harris-Ross and I then design a customized workshop for the client. Once on-site, our workshops usually run for about four hours, beginning with a pre-test, used to determine the participants' level of awareness about sexual harassment issues. The questions are very general—basically asking if participants know what it is and if they think it's prevalent in their workplace. The pre-test also helps us and management determine how much understanding increases by workshop's end. Typically, we find that workshop attendees are generally unaware of what sexual harassment is and of how prevalent it is in their own workplace.

Next we give a verbal presentation, beginning with a basic definition of sexual harassment and what it typically costs organizations in terms of litigation, employee turnover, increased absenteeism, lowered productivity, etc. This usually dampens the frivolous attitude that some male participants bring with them ("Oh great, a sexual harassment workshop. Now I can learn to do it better!").

We also stress that while most harassers are men, most men are not harassers. Aside from the obvious truth of that statement, articulating it helps create a nonthreatening environment conducive to learning.

Other issues we cover include:

- how to recognize sexual harassment
- examples of sexual harassment
- myths surrounding the issue (e.g., she caused it by what she was wearing)
- consequences of the behavior—for the target and for the offender—in emotional, legal, and financial terms
- what typically happens when a complaint is made, formally and informally
- pertinent city, state, and work-related laws and regulations

In workshops specifically designed for managers, we also cover sexual harassment policies, procedures, and prevention strategies.

Our workshops may include videos, case studies, and role-playing activities. After the role-playing scenarios, we discuss the responses and attitudes revealed, and explore alternative responses. We ask whether the situation could have been resolved less antagonistically. If so, how? What went wrong?

In some cases, clients ask us to conduct further research to uncover specific problem areas. In these instances, we ask workshop participants to complete a detailed questionnaire on relationships within the particular company, the environment, general climate toward women, workplace morale, etc. Questionnaires are returned anonymously to ensure confidentiality.

Sample questions might include:

- Have *you* experienced sexual harassment on the job?
- Have you witnessed it?
- If so, was the incident reported? Why or why not?
- What was the outcome?
- How did you feel about it?
- Are sexual/racial jokes told and tolerated?
- Under what circumstances?
- What is your reaction to them?
- Do you participate?
- Do you believe women and men are treated differently?
- If so, how?
- Do you perceive any resentment between men and women in the company?
- If so, to what do you attribute it?

Based on responses to these questions, the company has a clearer idea of what's going on in their workplace. From that knowledge, further workshops, guidelines, policies, and plans for implementation can take place.

What You Always Wanted to Know, But Were Afraid to Ask

Throughout our workshops, we encourage participants to ask questions. And they do! Here are a few of the most commonly asked, along with our answers:

Q: What if someone makes a false complaint?

A: Workers have little to gain from filing a false charge. The complainer is putting him/herself in a position to be ridiculed, disbelieved, gossiped about, and even fired. However, if someone does press false charges, he/she should be liable to the same disciplinary procedures as a harasser might be, including reprimand, demotion, transfer, or termination. It is the company's responsibility to protect the rights of *all* its employees.

Q: If I ask someone out on a date, is that sexual harassment? Where does it cross the line?

A: If the attraction between two people is mutual and the date is welcomed, clearly we're not talking sexual harassment here. That said, and for reasons detailed earlier, we still don't encourage interoffice dating.

Similarly, if you approach someone for a date and he/she says no and it ends there, it's not sexual harassment. But, if you persist and create an offensive or uncomfortable atmosphere for your coworker, then you've crossed the line to sexual harassment. Watch for signals that you are making someone uncomfortable, and if you are unsure, ask.

Q: If I put my arm around someone, or touch her, is that sexual harassment?

A: Could be. Look for signals both verbal and nonverbal. If you rest your hand on someone's shoulder and she/he shrugs it off, you've been sent a message—heed it. You are being told that she/he is uncomfortable and wants you to stop. Be aware, however, that some women—especially those who are younger or further down the career ladder—may smile out of embarrassment or discomfort, but in no way mean to encourage you.

Q: Why do some women get bent out of shape if I call them "honey" or "dear"?

A: It's demeaning. Every employee has a name. Use it.

Q: What should I do if sexual harassment happens to me?

A: Try to determine whether it really *is* sexual harassment. Then, if you can summon up the courage, approach the offender and tell him/ her it makes you uncomfortable and to please stop. If the behavior continues, check the company policies as to procedure. If there are none, go to your supervisor or the appropriate designated person. Obviously, I suggest you read books like this one for more complete advice. (Refer to chapter 5.)

Q: What's the best way to approach my supervisor about a harassment complaint?

A: Clearly and dispassionately—if at all possible (and I am the first one to understand that it might not be). As best you can, make three points:

1. This is what happened (the exact circumstance and who was involved).
2. This is how I'm feeling (scared, humiliated, etc.).
3. This is what I want to happen (an investigation, the person to be reprimanded/transferred, etc.). If you receive no satisfaction, I suggest documenting your experiences and gathering as much information on the subject as possible—again, through books like this—to determine your options.

Wrapping It Up

We end the workshop by questioning our attendees to help them express their feelings about what they've just seen and heard. Usually this results in spirited and rewarding discussions, which we try to end on a positive note.

We don't get through to everyone. I'm the first to admit that attitudes don't change overnight—much less during a four-hour workshop, no matter how compelling. Some attendees leave thinking, "Well, now that we've been through this, we can forget all about sexual harassment." Of course, strong and committed management—and much follow-up discussion of policies—can do a lot to overcome these attitudes.

Sample Harassment Policies

Although I strongly encourage you to develop your own policies—indigenous to your company and with input from management—it can be helpful to review what others have done. Here are two that are currently in effect, one developed by the Detroit Police Department *after* my own case, the other the nationally-recognized policy developed by the megacorporation, AT&T.

Sexual Harassment Policy of the Detroit Police Department

Federal law contains the following definition of sexual harassment, which is specifically incorporated into department policy. Unwelcome sexual advances, requests for sexual favors and other verbal and physical conduct of a sexual nature constitute sexual harassment when:

1. Submission to such conduct is made either explicitly or implicitly a term or condition of an individual's employment.
2. Submission to or rejection of such conduct by an individual is used as the basis for employment decisions affecting such individual, or ...
3. Such conduct has the purpose or effect of unreasonably interfering with an individual's work performance or creating an intimidating, hostile or offensive working environment.

Investigatory Procedures

In addition to any other complaint or discipline procedure provided in department policy, any person believing that they have been subject to discrimination or harassment on the basis of their race, creed, sex, or national origin, may forward a complaint, either directly or through official channels, to the Equal Opportunity Coordinator, who will conduct a complete investigation into the complaint and provide a timely investigatory report to the Chief of Police concerning the validity of the complaint, and the initiation of appropriate disciplinary charges. The complaining member shall be provided with a written disposition of the investigation.

Nothing in this policy relieves individual commanding officers or supervisors from taking immediate and appropriate corrective action in dealing with any violation of the rules and regulations of the Detroit Police Department.

AT&T Sexual Harassment Policy

It is Company policy that all employees have a right to work in an environment free of discrimination, which encompasses freedom from sexual harassment of its employees in any form.

Specifically, no supervisor shall threaten or insinuate, either explicitly or implicitly, that an employee's submission to or rejection of sexual advances will in any way influence any personnel decision regarding that employee's employment, wages, advancement, assigned duties, shifts, or any other condition of employment or career development.

Other sexually harassing conduct in the workplace which may create an offensive work environment, whether it be in the form of physical or verbal harassment, and regardless of whether committed by supervisory or nonsupervisory personnel, is also prohibited. This includes, but is not limited to: repeated offensive or unwelcome sexual flirtations, advances, propositions; continual or repeated verbal abuse of a sexual nature; graphic verbal commentaries about an individual's body; sexually degrading words used to describe an individual; and the display in the workplace of sexually suggestive objects or pictures.

An employee who believes that he or she is being harassed should:

- Carefully consider whether the conduct in question is harassment
- Confront the person responsible and request that the conduct cease
- If the problem is not resolved, take the complaint through the lines of supervision, beginning with the employee's own supervisor
- If this is not desirable, appropriate, or possible, discuss the complaint with the applicable AT&T EOAA representative.

Sexual harassment in the workplace by any employee:

- Will result in disciplinary action up to and including dismissal and
- May lead to personal, legal and financial liability.

Eight Mistakes for Managers to Avoid When Handling a Sexual Harassment Allegation

- Not taking an allegation seriously because it's not a formal complaint, resenting the complainant, or seeing the incident as a nuisance.
- Not taking an allegation seriously because of feelings that that target "asked for it" by her style of dress or behavior.
- Not taking an allegation seriously because it seems to result from a soured relationship or because it seems to be a personal matter between two people.
- Trying to resolve the situation yourself, rather than consulting EEO, human resource, or legal department personnel.
- Deciding that the best way to handle a charge is by ignoring it, downplaying it, trying to talk the target out of taking action, or by transferring or dismissing her.
- Acting before an investigation is complete, for example, by disciplining one party prematurely or by making a decision based on heresay.
- Interfering with an investigation because: "I know Tom and he'd never do that" or because "She's just out to ruin Joe's career or to get money from the company."
- Believing that sexual jokes and innuendos and sexually-charged behavior are natural in the workplace and employees who don't like it should leave.

A Manager's Checklist for Preventing Sexual Harassment

1. Develop a specific policy against sexual harassment.
   _____ Does your company have such a policy?
   _____ Has it been disseminated to employees?
   _____ Is there a procedure to inform new employees of the policy?

2. Develop specific procedures—both formal and informal—to handle sexual harassment complaints.

_____Does your company have such procedures?

_____Has information about the procedures been disseminated to employees?

_____ Is at least one person outside the normal chain of command designated to handle complaints?

_____Have similar procedures been incorporated into union contracts?

3. Develop a code of conduct for all employees.

_____ Is sexual harassment referred to in the employee manual or code of conduct?

_____ Does the manual contain policy language regarding sexual harassment?

_____ Is sexual harassment discussed during training or orientation meetings?

_____Are policies well publicized?

_____Does the code of conduct include guidelines for behavior in the office, at conferences, parties, etc.?

4. Sensitize employees to the issue of sexual harassment.

_____ Has there been a training program for managers?

_____ Has there been a training program for line employees?

FOURTEEN

Educating Our Children: They Get Harassed, Too

We generally think of sexual harassment as offensive behavior that one adult forces upon another—something that happens in the workplace. We don't associate it with our children, but we should. Kids are people, too: they harass and get harassed. Incidents of sexual harassment happen every day in our children's schools—from the elementary level all the way up through college. It is just as prevalent and just as damaging as workplace harassment. In fact, as you read through this chapter and begin to see what sexual harassment *is* among our young, I'll bet you'll start to remember incidents from your own growing-up years—times when you were made to feel bad or humiliated because of your sex. It's doubtful that any of us would have called it sexual harassment back then—more likely, we felt it was just part of growing up, a part that sent egos tumbling down. But anytime a girl has to cross the street to avoid a group of boys because they yell demeaning, sexual comments at her, that is sexual harassment. Any time a boy gets pointed at in the school locker room because he hasn't matured as quickly as his friends, *that* is sexual harassment. And it's still about power, not sex.

In some ways, I consider this to be the most important chapter of this book. For the better we can teach our children respect for themselves and others, the further along we will be toward eliminating sexual harassment. Ultimately, it is what we do—or don't do—as parents and educators that will determine whether we raise a generation of sexual harassers or a generation of men and women who can work and live together on equal terms.

Where It Happens

As yet, no national surveys have measured the scope of sexual harassment in the schools, but from the growing number of reported incidents, it's clear that it happens not just in inner-city schools, but in well-funded, "nice" suburban districts as well. It happens in the stairwells, cafeterias, hallways, bathrooms, darkrooms, and outside on school grounds. The vast majority of cases involve peer-to-peer harassment—kids harassing other kids. A smaller proportion occurs between students and their teachers or other school personnel. As you might guess, at this state it's mostly boys harassing girls. But girls also target boys, and adolescents of both sexes have been known to harass peers who seem weak, homosexual, or effeminate. All adolescents are insecure. Sometimes the only way they can feel good about themselves is by putting another down, by showing that they are more powerful than the victim—and sometimes the form it takes is sexual harassment.

Examples

- An eighth-grade girl in an auto-mechanics class is constantly subjected to humiliating, dirty, sexist jokes and comments. The shop teacher hears these comments but never intervenes. The girl never says a word to anyone but suddenly drops the class.
- A high-school girl refuses a classmate's sexual advances on a date. Angered, he starts a rumor about her in school that she is a skank and a slut. Other guys pick up on it, making her the object of humiliation.
- For more than a year, a shy sophomore is continually bothered by a male student who constantly leers at her, follows her, touches her, and says crude, humiliating things to her. She is too embarrassed to say anything to her teachers or principal to get the boy to stop.

- On a bet, a junior high school student flings a girl's skirt over her head. He wins twenty-five dollars from his friends.
- A well-developed fifth grader wears a bra. The boys take turns running up behind her and snapping the back of her bra.
- A girl in a skirt stands at the top of the stairwell. A boy summons all his friends to stand at the bottom and look up her skirt.
- A boy who is not yet interested in girls is picked on by his peers, who tell him he must be gay. He wonders if it's true.
- Passing in the hallway to change classes, a boy reaches out and grabs a girl's breast. She feels singled out and humiliated, certain the entire school saw what happened. She can think about nothing else all day long and fails a test she had been completely prepared for.
- A high schooler is harassed by the band director, who touches her during practice and hints of his interest in having sex with her when the band travels to a concert date. The student is courageous enough to complain to the principal, but he doesn't believe her. He tells her the band director has an unblemished record, so she must have imagined it.
- Sexual harassment can lead to more serious crimes. An English teacher has a six-month sexual relationship with a student who was thirteen when the liaison began; he is sentenced to ten years in prison.
- A twelve-year-old is sexually assaulted by three boys who force her to perform oral sex in the school's basement boiler room. The child tells a teacher, who informs the principal. The principal doubts the girl's story and refuses to call the boys in for discipline.

Incredible and revolting as some of these stories sound, they are all true. Worse, they're the tip of the iceberg; for each one that is reported, hundreds more go unreported.

I, too, was the target of sexual harassment in my high school, and although it was an isolated incident, I still remember clearly the overwhelming sense of shame and embarrassment I felt afterwards. During my senior year, I was a lab assistant for my science teacher. He was a particularly sympathetic and warm-hearted man who always seemed to have time for my questions and to lend a sympathetic ear to my problems. Coming from the family I did, I appreciated his attentiveness. After working with him for a few months, I felt I could trust him.

One day, he invited me to ride downstairs in the teachers' elevator to my next class with him. After the doors closed, he suddenly pushed the Stop button and was all over me, grabbing me, trying to kiss me and fondle my breasts. I freaked out, started to shake uncontrollably, and broke down crying. I begged him to stop, and he did. I couldn't believe this was happening to me, that one of the few adults I'd allowed myself to trust could betray me this way and make me feel so bad. Reporting the incident never occurred to me. I didn't know what to do about it. Since he never mentioned it, I continued to work for him and just pretended the whole thing never happened, but I could never look him in the eye again. And a part of me felt dirty and guilty—as though what happened was my fault.

Schools Can Be "Hostile Environments"

These sorts of incidents—both the relatively "minor" ones and the criminal examples—have profound effects on their victims, teenagers whose egos and self-images are developing and still very fragile. Many suffer from a deep and lasting sense of shame, powerlessness, and anger. Self-confidence collapses, and physical symptoms, such as insomnia and listlessness, often appear. Even when there is no physical assault, the effects can be as severe as if one had occurred.

Sexual harassment always creates an atmosphere of intimidation. If you are intimidated in school, your ability to learn is the first thing that's impaired. Young people who are harassed are often made so uncomfortable they cannot concentrate. As in the workplace, the school-age victim becomes fixated on avoiding the harasser and even certain areas of the school building or grounds. She/he may start missing classes—the quality of her/his work can't help but suffer. That can and has led to victims transferring to other schools, dropping classes, even dropping out of school completely. And to me, that's a tragedy. Bystanders become unwitting victims. Students who witness or hear of the harassment frequently also feel forced to change *their* behavior—avoiding certain hallways, keeping a low profile, anything—to avoid becoming a direct target.

Ultimately, sexual harassment creates a "hostile environment," exactly what is referred to in the EEOC workplace guidelines. It sets up a situation where girls cannot get the equal education they are entitled to. Because of this, sexual harassment in schools is considered a form of discrimination and is illegal under state and federal law.

In 1992, the U.S. Supreme Court put teeth into a twenty-year-old federal law banning sexual discrimination in schools—including harassment—by allowing victims to collect damages from school districts. Sometimes it takes the threat of being hit in the pocketbook to wake people up to a serious problem.

How to Recognize Harassment

The first step toward preventing sexual harassment is to teach children what it is and why it's so destructive. This can and should be done on two fronts—in the home and at school. Many kids simply endure harassing behavior because they don't realize what it is. They think it's just something they *have* to go through. As one Montana high school student said after a school-sponsored session on the problem, "There were a lot of things I never realized were sexual harassment, which I would let go by. Now I'm more aware of things like rude comments, and I'll say something."

Other adolescents confuse sexual harassment with flirting. While it varies from each individual, we need to point out the difference: flirting feels good, sexual harassment makes people feel bad. It makes them feel ashamed, embarrassed, trapped, uncomfortable, or uncertain inside.

We should tell our kids, simply, that sexual harassment is unwanted sexual attention. It includes:

- touching, grabbing or, rubbing up against someone
- making crude or degrading personal remarks about someone's body, and similar sexual remarks or suggestions
- sexually offensive behavior, jokes, notes, graffiti
- leering stares
- sexual intimidation
- physical sexual assaults (a criminal offense)

Sexual harassment is a put-down—even in its mildest form. It's taking pleasure in someone else's pain or discomfort. It hurts people and makes them feel bad. That's what makes it wrong.

Peer Influence

Something else we should teach our kids to look out for is the role of peers. Often when harassment occurs, a third group of people is involved, the bystanders—other kids who are witnesses or who hear rumors. We can emphasize that the reaction of witnesses can either help stop sexual harassment in its tracks, or make it a whole lot worse.

That's why it's so important to stress that young people have a responsibility—even when it's someone else being harassed—to get involved. At the very least, they should:

- not go along with this type of behavior
- not do or say anything that will encourage the harasser

Teen harassers are often looking for approval and encouragement. Young people should be cautioned not to giggle or stare at the person being harassed, or add more jokes or gossip about what happened. That only makes the situation worse.

More than that, young people should be encouraged to speak out against harassment when they see it. And they should be taught to feel disgust when they witness sexual harassment, and should say, "I don't think that's funny," or tell the harasser to stop.

It Begins in the Home

If you're serious about curtailing sexual harassment, begin in your own home. Think about the messages your children receive there. Have you scrutinized your own behavior and attitudes lately? Do you:

- make comments to your son like "She's just a girl," as if being a girl is reason enough to be discounted? Are you teaching your daughter to value a guy's opinion more than a girl's—including her own?
- permit women to be regarded as physical objects in your home? Are sexually explicit magazines, or cable-TV channels accessible to your kids?
- teach your children to respect women, or is the general attitude in your home one of woman-bashing or mean-spiritedness

toward women? What example does your relationship with your spouse or partner set?
- lead your daughter to believe that any attention from a guy—even abusive attention—is better than none at all? Are you teaching her to smile or be passive, even when she's being put down?

Your example and the standards you set in your home are critically influential. If, for example, you are in an emotionally or physically abusive relationship, your message to your son is that abuse—including sexual harassment—is permissible. Your message to your daughter is that abuse and harassment is what she should expect, and what she deserves. (If you are in an abusive relationship, take steps to change it. Otherwise, get out. Do it for your children's sake.)

Dress Code

Although the older your children are, the less influence you wield over what they wear, still, a little guidance can make a big difference. Many teens—especially girls—eagerly adopt the latest clothing, makeup, and hairstyles, which are often copied from music videos. Many are overtly sexual and demeaning. Although nothing gives a boy the right to sexually harass a girl, you can help your daughter understand that the way she carries herself, dresses, even how she talks—especially if she uses crude language—influences how a guy responds to her. It may send signals to potential harassers that she is "game."

To your son, you should strongly point out that no matter how someone dresses or acts doesn't make sexual harassment okay.

Body-Language Signals

Many teenage boys not only misinterpret the fashion statements girls make, they also misinterpret nonverbal signals. For generations, girls have been raised to be "nice," to smile even when they are unhappy. The result is that girls who are being harassed may give an embarrassed smile or simply keep quiet—thinking that silence indicates disapproval. The unfortunate result is that even when a girl thinks she's sending out a clear signal for a guy to stop bothering her, he simply may not get it.

Teach your daughter to be as assertive as possible, to state her "no" messages in unmistakable terms. Teach your son, meanwhile, to be alert to another person's discomfort and nonverbal signals.

Above all, what girls need to hear from their parents is that they don't have to put up with any behavior that makes them feel uncomfortable sexually. Many girls are testing their desirability, and having guys find them attractive becomes extremely important— even at the cost of putting up with all sorts of negative behavior. Harassers take advantage of this.

By teaching your children that someone who humiliates them or hurts them isn't the kind of person they want to attract, you are doing them a great service. (For girls, this message is especially potent coming from a father or adult male whom they respect and admire.) The key is to teach our children to treat themselves respectfully and to demand respect from others.

For the Boys

Boys who have empathy, who have learned to value and respect others, seldom become harassers. It's your responsibility to teach your son these qualities as soon as he is old enough to understand.

At puberty, boys normally start to regard girls differently than they did before. The message they get from their peers is that girls are no longer people, but rather, objects to be "conquered." (I believe the current term is "nailed.") Feeling a sense of empathy from an early age will help them get past this stage quickly. You can help by pointing out when women are portrayed negatively on TV, so there's less chance a child will accept it as normal behavior. When you observe women being humiliated or harassed, ask your son how he would feel if the target was someone he cared about and respected— his mom or little sister, for example.

Help him understand that harassment is putting someone down for something she can't control. People cannot change whether they are male or female. A girl cannot (without surgery) control the size of her breasts. Ask your son to imagine how he would feel if someone looked at his testicles and called him "small balls" or "stick dick." He'd probably feel ashamed of his body. Explain to him that girls who are harassed feel exactly the same way.

Ignorance Isn't Bliss

Overwhelmingly, schools have avoided dealing with the issue of sexual harassment. The general thinking is that if administrators or teachers address the issue, they are admitting their school has a problem. Ignoring it has been the standard solution.

This attitude has not only allowed sexual harassment in the schools to fester, it has also sent a strong and destructive message to students. When those in authority condone, ignore, or downplay sexual harassment, they are teaching that victims—usually girls—don't count, that they are not equal, that boys have more power in this area, and that it's okay for girls to be the objects of scorn.

It's not that teachers and administrators are uncaring or cruel—most simply aren't aware of the scope of the problem. Some teachers understand how destructive sexual harassment can be, but they don't feel equipped to discipline the offenders, or they don't know whether they'll be backed up by administrators. Whatever their reasoning, the sad fact is that in many schools, a student caught smoking in the hallway is punished more severely than is a sexual harasser.

There is some good news on the school front. A growing number of states, Minnesota, for example, are mandating that schools devise and implement sexual harassment policies. Some school districts are recognizing the importance of having clear policies, whether states require them or not. Additionally, state laws are offering a variety of recourses for victims of sexual harassment in the schools, as evidenced by the following true story.

The Katy Lyle Case

Katy Lyle was a sophomore in a Duluth, Minnesota, high school when graffiti about her started appearing in one of the boys' bathrooms, phrases like "Katy Lyle is a whore" and worse. Katy, who described herself as a "music geek," did not even date actively at that point.

When friends told her about the graffiti, Katy told a teacher and a counselor about it. They promised to have the graffiti cleaned off from what had become known as "the Katy Stall." Three months later, it was still there, along with additional and increasingly vulgar things about her. The situation continued throughout Katy's sophomore and junior year, despite attempts by Katy and her parents to force the school to clean it up. In all, the Lyles contacted the school at least sixteen times. Each time, the administration promised to do something about it, and each time, the Lyles believed them. Still, nothing changed.

The effects on Katy were devastating. Most of her classmates would having nothing to do with her. Boys avoided her. People constantly made comments. She was a pariah and a laughingstock at her school. Katy was a former honor student; her grades plummeted.

Katy and her family finally filed a complaint with the Minnesota Department of Human Rights. The case was settled in 1991: Katy won $15,000 and the school agreed to educate the students on harassment and make sure the stalls were graffiti-free. "It was almost funny how fast the graffiti was cleaned up after the suit was filed," Katy remarked to a reporter.

What Schools Can Do

Katy's experience and those of other students who encounter stonewalling by teachers and administrators point up the need for better education about sexual harassment all around. Just as there must be guidelines in the workplace, I feel strongly that there must be official school policies against sexual harassment. Additionally, a curriculum should be devised and implemented in the classroom, so we can properly educate our children about this issue.

Here are a few suggestions detailing what schools can do:

1. Decide to educate teachers, staff, and students about sexual harassment and how to prevent it. This education should be an ongoing process—not a one-time deal.
2. Workshops and training sessions should be conducted for all staff. All adults within the school should be trained to identify sexual harassment, understand why it's detrimental, and be given techniques for prevention. The sessions should also include ways to work this issue into the curriculum.

3. All schools, at every level, should have a clearly written policy against sexual harassment of all types, whether it's peer-to-peer or adult–student. Schools should also devise formal and informal procedures to deal with the problem.

In peer-to-peer harassment, informal resolutions are generally all that's needed. School policy could demand a simple written and verbal apology from the harasser to the victim. A conference could also be called between the victim, the harasser, a teacher, and possibly the harasser's parents, to ensure that the harasser understands what the problem is and promises to stop the offending behavior. Depending on the severity of the offense, other disciplinary actions might include detentions, requiring research on sexual harassment, and for repeat offenders, suspension or expulsion.

Everyone at the school—all faculty and students—should be made aware of the policy, through memos, posters, and flyers. It should be covered in student and employee handbooks as well as the school newspaper. Schools should also be sure that any newcomers to the system are informed of the policy.

Clear, enforceable policies prohibiting sexual harassment are to the school's advantage, but more important, they help provide an atmosphere conducive to learning for all students— male and female.

4. Administrators should designate a few well-known adults to act as harassment-complaint managers. These adults might include a teacher, a guidance counselor, and an administrator. Students should know who these people are.

5. Information regarding sexual harassment should be incorporated into the curriculum. This can be done in a variety of classes, such as social studies (units on current events), legal education, sex education, and health classes.

Topics to cover regarding sexual harassment include:

- what it is
- why it happens
- how it hurts
- that harassers are breaking the law
- how to prevent or handle harassment

When discussing why harassment occurs, it can be helpful for kids to also look at the harasser's point of view—and to note that one incident of harassment may be the result of misunderstanding. The juvenile harasser may be unaware that he's really hurting someone. He may think it's funny, or he may be trying to get her to like him. On the other hand, it's also possible that he may be angry and feel that his target "deserves" to be put down.

Another tactic is in-class assertiveness-training and role-playing. Using these techniques, teachers can help students overcome the feeling that harassment is their fault, or that others will laugh at them, think they're wimps, or accuse them of having no sense of humor if they report harassment.

Above all, teachers can help their students deal with harassment—and other forms of sexual/racial abuse or coercion—by teaching them to trust their feelings. Students, especially girls, need to know that if certain remarks or actions make them uncomfortable, it's their right to have them stopped.

6. Encourage students to set up awareness—or rap—sessions of their own to talk about their perceptions of sexual harassment. Opening the lines of communication between girls and boys helps them to understand each other's different preconceptions and expectations, and can help each understand what it's like to be in the other's shoes.

Teachers can encourage students to track or survey the extent of sexual harassment in the school and report it in the school newspaper, or even set up peer-support groups. (This can be especially helpful in vocational schools for girls studying non-traditional subjects such as auto mechanics.)

Steps to Take When Harassment Occurs

Despite our best efforts at prevention, sexual harassment will still occur. Here are some tips you can give your child on how to deal with it. As you'll see, they're not so very different from the steps we as adults can take.

1. Talk to the tormentor right away. Tell him/her that this behavior is unacceptable.

2. Keep a journal. Write down what happened, when and where it happened, who witnessed it, how it made you feel, and what you did about it.
3. Write a letter to the harasser. Explain exactly what happened, the fact that it is unacceptable, and what the consequences will be if the behavior continues ("I will report you to the dean"). Deliver it in school to the harasser with an adult witness present.
4. Most important, tell somebody about it—your parents, teachers, guidance counselor, cleric, an adult you trust.

If, however, a child is having obvious trouble handling it on his/her own, parental intervention is necessary. As in the workplace, going up the chain of command is the proper strategy here. Assuming it's an in-school problem, start by talking to teachers, the guidance department, and then the principal. If none of those measures helps, the next step is to make a report to the board of education, first on a local level, and if that doesn't resolve the matter, on a state level. Filing a claim with the state human rights commission would be next, then the EEOC, and if it comes to it, hiring an attorney, and perhaps going to the press. Only in the most dire cases will you ever have to go *that* far, but when it comes to protecting the rights of our children, we go as far as we have to.

FIFTEEN

Educating Ourselves:
"He Said, She Heard"

Formulating rules for companies to follow or teaching our children will do very little good unless we also change *our* ways of thinking about and dealing with one another. Only then can we hope to eradicate sexual harassment and other gender-driven indignities from our lives once and for all.

Without ignoring the very real—and important—differences between men and women, we need to relearn the language when some of us speak to each other. We need to learn to address one another in a way that is not demeaning or degrading; we need to understand that sometimes, although our intentions are innocent, our words do indeed establish a hierarchy that is often completely inappropriate, and especially so in the workplace. We need to understand that our words can not only hurt, but some of those words, in certain situations, are against the law. Some gestures and physical contacts are illegal. Sometimes, we don't recognize our own hidden agendas, our attitudes behind our words and gestures. What men say is not always what women hear. What men mean is not always what they thought they said. Education for ourselves is key.

WHAT MEN NEED TO LEARN

You're Not Being Friendly—You're Being Condescending

Judge Robert Beezer, of the Ninth U.S. Circuit Court in California, put it this way: "Conduct that many men consider unobjectionable may offend women."

I'd say that's the understatement of the year.

Let's take it from the mildest form of conduct that many men find *un*objectionable: addressing women in the workplace as "honey," or "sweetie," or "dollface," or "darling," as in, "Honey, could you get that file for me?" Or "So what did you think of that proposal, sweetie?"

I completely understand that many men, especially those over fifty, might see absolutely nothing objectionable about using "terms of endearment." Men I have spoken to insist they are just being friendly to their female coworkers and mean nothing untoward. I challenge them, "Have you ever considered asking how a female colleague *feels* when she is addressed in that manner?" For the most part, none have thought to ask. Well, I'll tell you: women feel instantly demoted.

Words are powerful; they convey power (yours) *and* powerlessness (theirs). Just bringing a simple endearment—a word you might very well use with your wife, mother, or sister—into the workplace is condescending and manipulative. It reduces a coworker, whether she is a surgeon or a secretary, to a status lower than your own. Consider addressing a male colleague this way: "Hey, little guy, bring me that file," or "So, big fella, what did you think of that proposal?" You would not dream of speaking that way to a grown male, and certainly not to any man in the office, even a lowly gofer or mailroom clerk. It is offensive to speak to women as though they were children. Just like men, women have *names*. Use them.

My advice: Think before you speak. Think about what you're saying. Think about what you really mean. Think about how you really *feel*. Are you resentful toward women in the workplace? Would you really like to take them down a peg or two? It's okay to admit that to yourself and deal with it privately. In fact, understanding your own agenda is a real first step toward educating yourself. It is not okay, however, to allow that attitude out in a public arena.

Q: Okay, it's demeaning, it's demoting, it's condescending. But is it sexual harassment? C'mon, can I really be prosecuted for calling my secretary "honey"?

A: No, you probably wouldn't be prosecuted, but it can be a form of sexual harassment. Ask your secretary how she feels—I'd bet dollars to doughnuts, although she may have felt uncomfortable saying anything to you, she'd really prefer to be called by her name. Wouldn't you?

You're Not Showing Deference—You're Creating Difference

Many men, again especially those of a certain age, were brought up with two vocabularies, one to use among men, the other for mixed company. Cursing, when "among the guys," is an often accepted way to converse. When women are present, however, many men will refrain from using expletives. Private attitudes are one thing and not my business. When they carry over to a business situation and create problems attached to sexual harassment, that *is* my business.

Many women—and some men, too—find cursing offensive. To keep doing it after you've been asked to stop is sexual harassment. But there's another, more subtle, and therefore insidious way men use cursing around female coworkers. Disguised as good manners, it masks a hidden agenda. Let's consider a business meeting around a conference table. A male colleague lets loose with an expletive, and then turns to the nearest female and says, "Pardon my French" or "Pardon my language," apparently deferring to the "lady" sitting among the men. What he has in effect done is to discriminate subtly between the sexes, pointing out that the "fairer," or "weaker" sex must be shielded from naughty language. In fact, what she should be shielded from is being singled out as different from the men...as someone who might have some brilliant business strategies to bring to the table, but (wink, wink) hey, guys, how seriously can we really take her? After all, she's just a *girl* who shouldn't even be exposed to a curse word. We just made *that* clear.

My advice: Cursing is always inappropriate at work. And again, think about what's really motivating the words that come out of your mouth.

You're Not Complimenting Her—You're Humiliating Her

While using terms of endearment and/or expletives may still seem relatively harmless to many men, I think everyone can understand why drawing attention to a woman's body is inappropriate in the workplace. Done once, it's humiliating. Done over and over again, it's sexual harassment. Talking at a woman's chest instead of to her face is telling her that she is valued for her body, not her mind. Look at it this way: if your boss (male or female) eyeballed your crotch while speaking to you, do you think he/she would really be paying attention to what's on your mind? Chances are you'd know you were being ignored, and you'd feel... humiliated. That's how she feels.

What if she's wearing a tight-fitting dress? What if she's... *asking* for it? That's what people used to say about rape victims. It didn't wash in that circumstance, and it doesn't wash in this one. I don't think women should wear tight-fitting tops or short skirts to the workplace, but even when they do, it doesn't give men the right to harass. That's her mistake; don't make it yours.

Q: Does that mean I can't even compliment a woman at work on how she looks without being accused of harassment?

A: There's a way of saying "That's a nice dress" without meaning "I love the way that dress hugs your hips." And I think men know that.

He Said, She Heard

He said: "I missed your last remarks. I was admiring your physical assets rather than your intellectual ones."

He thought he meant: A compliment. Don't all women want to be told they are physically attractive?

She heard: What I think or say has no merit around here. A push-up bra would get me further in this company than a brilliant idea.

What he really meant: Not only could a woman not *have* a worthwhile idea, I'm gonna let her know it.

She knew exactly what he really meant.

What Do These Women Really Want?

Most women in the workplace don't want to be discriminated against, or held on a pedestal. They don't want to be "one of the guys."

They want to be judged on their competence and allowed to display that competence in the same way as anyone else in the company.

What do women *really* want? They want to be regarded as and judged as *one of the workers*.

WHAT WOMEN NEED TO LEARN

They're Following Old Patterns of Behavior

Some men use sexual language and imagery all the time and rarely stop to think about it. Although I don't condone their behavior, what I think is important for women to recognize is that some men—older men, especially—entered the workplace before the age of enlightenment. There was a time, not so long ago, when sexual teasing and innuendo was accepted. I'm not saying that it was welcomed by women—I'm sure for the most part it wasn't—but there was a time when it was simply status quo. Not only did men routinely engage in what they thought was friendly banter, it was expected. From the messages they got from society, from their role models at home, teachers in school, and mentors in the workplace, that was the way men and women were supposed to relate to each other. That's how men proved to their peers that they were real men, one of the guys. Everyone understood the rules of the game.

These men have no sense that there's anything wrong. They don't even think about it. They don't relate what they're doing to the Thomas–Hill hearings or sexual harassment headlines in the news. It just seems natural to use endearments with women, to shield them from curses, and compliment them on their sexy looks. Besides, they've been doing it for years, and no one's brought *them* up on any charges.

I'm not condoning this rationale, but I think it pays to understand where it might be coming from in certain cases. Deciding how to handle it is made easier by recognizing that most men are not deliberate sexual harassers. While their words are *not* harmless, while it isn't okay, most men are not hard-core harassers. Once they have been enlightened, once they can understand the negative effect they have on women, they should be able to curb their behavior. Most do.

My advice: They say you can't teach an old dog new tricks, but it's time to try. You might diplomatically ask to be addressed by your name. Let your fifty-something male colleagues know you aren't comfortable with "sweetie," even though you realize that's their way of being informal.

"I Don't Understand These New Rules"

Women need to realize that after these "new tricks" are pointed out, the "old dogs" may react with confusion and/or straight-out resentment. Most people resist change, especially if the old way worked well enough for them! (If it ain't broke, don't fix it.) They may profess to be completely confused—"But we treat our girls so well here!"—and proclaim not to understand how demeaning that is.

Then there's the resentment of having suddenly to watch their language, of having to watch where they put their hands, of being pressured into thinking about their true motivations.

Again, these are not reasons to take a giant step backward and forget about the issue of sexual harassment, but it is cathartic to comprehend where certain men are coming from. Forging a new understanding between men and women can only help in the long run.

Vive la Différence!

To men who shout, *"Vive la différence!"*—meaning that men and women were *not* created the same, were never meant to *be* the same, that pretending they *are* the same robs us of one of life's greatest pleasures—I say that one thing has nothing to do with the other. I say, "Vive la individuality!" Let's get to know and celebrate each other as people, not as genders or races or religions. Relations between the sexes, when healthy and equal, are indeed among life's greatest pleasures and treasures; using one's power through sexuality to humiliate and demean the other is sick. But it's a disease that can be cured. All we have to do is want to cure it.

WHAT WE ALL NEED TO LEARN

The popular book *You Just Don't Understand,* by linguistics professor Deborah Tannen, is all about cross-communication between the sexes—what one means, the other doesn't always hear. Although Dr. Tannen doesn't specifically discuss sexual harassment, she points out some innate psychological differences between men and women. When expressed in communication, these differences *can,* and often *do,* leave the door open to misunderstanding and sexual harassment. That's why I think it's important for both men and women to recognize these differences.

After exhaustive research and study, Dr. Tannen concludes that boys are brought up to seek status by being in charge, to give orders for others to follow. Games boys play often involve direct conflict and challenge, like King of the Hill. Girls, on the other hand, are brought up to compromise, to get what they want through intimation and indirection, as opposed to intimidation. For girls, status is achieved by connection to others, by popularity. When girls play house, there are no winners and losers, only cooperative players. Girls want to be liked; boys want to be respected.

All of us bring our psychological makeup into the workplace with us. That is where it can create problems, especially when sexual harassment comes into the picture. If men are wired always to be thinking in terms of one-upmanship, it's easy to understand why words that put women down may come naturally. As Dr. Tannen points out, even when they refer to a female coworker as *feisty* or *spunky,* they are using words appropriate for describing a Pekingese—a small powerless pet. It undercuts and trivializes her competence. It's not far from here to get into a harassment arena.

When a woman is seen as an expert at something—*the* expert in a given situation—men commonly resent it. Knowing more than a man gives a woman superiority for that moment, and that's a place neither is traditionally comfortable with.

Men tell jokes—dirty or not—to claim center stage. In mixed

company, women seldom do. Again, they look for membership in a group, for camaraderie and sameness, not to set themselves apart.

If girls at play tend to avoid conflict, women at work often avoid confrontation. That's why for most women, trying to compromise, to accept what's going on, feels more natural than confronting a harasser head-on and immediately. It's *hard* to step out of your natural psychological habitat. I'm not saying you shouldn't—but I think we all need to acknowledge the reasons that it isn't easy. For many of us, we are fighting natural impulses.

In addition, women in business face a Catch-22 that again speaks to the way we are raised, the way we come pre-wired. When a woman is straightforward and completely businesslike, many people—men and women alike—resent her as arrogant and aggressive. When a woman doesn't continually smile, qualify her statements, cock her head charmingly, people perceive her as cold, hard, and competitive—not likable. And since women strive to be liked, that can be tough to accept. However, if a woman is seen as very feminine, engaging in traditional "womanly behavior," she may seem to accept being treated differently. And we already know how quickly *different* can lead to *demeaning*. Women don't want to lose their humanity, but they also don't want that humanity to be used against them.

Understanding Won't Make It Go Away

Knowing what psychological baggage we bring to the table—be it the conference table or the kitchen table—won't make the basic differences go away. Understanding, however, can go a long way toward banishing inappropriate, and certainly unlawful behavior.

We can acknowledge our different styles, intents, and perhaps even our hidden agendas. What we must not do is let them cross the line into sexual exploitation and harassment.

Men may have been brought up to seek respect, but in the workplace, and at school and at home, we *all* need to strive to respect each other—as colleagues and, more important, as people. What we all need to understand is that we are all of the same species. Men are (approximately) half the human race; women are half the human race. Women are not the weaker sex; men are not the stronger sex. [The race we need to win] is the one toward an equal humanity.

Furthermore, we all need to understand that any new understanding will take time. Generations of old information need to be reprocessed. The struggle to banish sexual harassment, to fight for equality for all people, on all levels, is an evolution, not a revolution.

Let's teach ourselves. Let's teach our children well.

Different Perceptions..."And the Survey Said..."

According to a USA Today poll, 67 percent of men said they would be complimented if propositioned by a woman. Only 17 percent of women said they'd be complimented if propositioned by a man.

The *New York Times* reported on the following scenario posed by Dr. Michelle Paludi of Hunter College:

A woman gets a job teaching at a university and her department chairman, a man, invites her to lunch to discuss her research. At lunch, he never mentions the research, but instead delves into her personal life. After a few such lunches, he invites her to dinner, and then for drinks. While they are having drinks he tries to fondle her.

Male and female students were asked: "When did the sexual harassment *start?*" Most of the *women* students said at the first lunch, when he discussed her private life as opposed to her work. Most of the *men* felt the sexual harassment began when he fondled her.

SIXTEEN

The Good News

Although we've got a long way to go toward curing sexual harassment, there *is* some good news on the homefront. We've come a long way from where we were just ten years ago.

A Greater Awareness

It was 1980 when the EEOC established its guidelines, and 1986 when the Supreme Court ruled on its first case. Still, during the Eighties, sexual harassment was hardly the number one topic of discussion at the office water cooler. I and so many others going through it got precious little support from our families and friends and precious little recognition from women's organizations or the media.

Then came the October 1991 Clarence Thomas confirmation hearings, which single-handedly lifted sexual harassment to the level of collective awareness it deserves. If for nothing else, we all must applaud the hearings for that. Sure, Judge Thomas was confirmed anyway; Professor Hill was treated like a criminal; and surveys showed that most Americans—male or female—didn't believe her. Still, the hearings got much of America talking and thinking about sexual harassment.

Once sexual harassment made it into the spotlight, the media focused upon it with customary intensity. Journalists wrote thought-

175

provoking investigative articles in newspapers as well as eye-catching cover stories in the major newsweeklies and in women's magazines. This trend is still going strong. As each article or book is read and absorbed by the public, it gets harder and harder for most people to say, "I don't believe this."

Books, such as this one, are being published to explain the situation, both in psychological and personal terms. Although many are targeted at management, others have been written to educate the public. Every time a book like this is read, another person gets the message.

Training videos for businesses are now proliferating. Used in conjunction with training workshops, they are an effective tool to teach management about the problem and how to deal with it.

Television and movies have jumped on the bandwagon. No matter how opportunistic they are, I welcome each new report and dramatization because it keeps sexual harassment in the spotlight. The TV newsmagazine, "Primetime Live," aired a compelling report about the subject in early 1992, which is now required viewing as part of management-training sessions at a large, international bank.

In May 1992, ABC broadcast a two-hour movie called *Sexual Advances*, starring Stephanie Zimbalist as an athletic-shoe-company executive who, when subjected to sexual harassment by her boss, suffers the emotional and career consequences of rebuffing him. Although the fictional story had formulaic aspects, it accurately depicted the bullying boss, the insensitive superior, the cowed co-workers, and the dilemma and downward spiraling of the victim. More people watch television than read newspapers, magazines, or books, so there's an awfully good chance that Americans saw and learned from *Sexual Advances* as much as they saw and learned from the Thomas–Hill hearings.

More People Are Speaking Up

Greater awareness of sexual harassment gives more individuals the courage to speak out publicly about their own private experiences. I applaud each and every one. And I urge more people to do the same: voices carry; each time a new voice is heard, one more person may be able to steel her will and say "No." And one more harasser may be stopped in his or her tracks.

It is not only personal tales that are being told. Employees are also speaking up about company images and policies that affect them indirectly. Female workers at Stroh's Brewery in St. Paul, Minnesota, banded together to express outrage about the company's "sexist, degrading" advertisements, featuring the scantily dressed Swedish Bikini Team. The ad campaign created an atmosphere hostile to women, they charged, and contributed to routine workplace harassment at the plant. These employees turned their outrage into action by filing a lawsuit against the company.

Negative publicity foisted upon companies whose employees tell the world of sexual harassment is very effective. Fewer companies find themselves able to ignore the issue. More companies are taking a proactive, preventive stance toward sexual harassment by setting policies, and by requiring management to enforce them and understand the consequences for resisting. Statistics reveal that 81 percent of Fortune 500 companies have sexual harassment training programs in effect in 1992, as opposed to 60 percent in 1988.

More Lawsuits Are Being Brought—And Won

Lawsuits are not fun. Nevertheless, it is good news that more victims have not only brought suits against their harassers, but *won*. That fact signifies a big change in public perception, and in the execution of justice.

A little over a decade ago, one of the first reported cases of sexual harassment went to trial in Arizona. Two female employees who had resigned from Bausch & Lomb, Inc., because of the repeated verbal and physical sexual advances of their supervisor, sued the company— and lost. The district court decided that the supervisor's harassment "appears to be nothing more than a personal proclivity, peculiarity or mannerism and that he was satisfying a personal urge." Further, the court felt that if it took action in this case, it would be opening the door for "a potential lawsuit every time any employee made amorous or sexually oriented advances toward another."

Times have changed dramatically in the courts. Today, victims of sexual harassment are winning money for back pay, pain and suffering, medical bills, and attorneys' fees. Some are winning big.

The more lawsuits brought and won, the more strongly our voices are heard; and the more likely employers will do everything in their power to avoid being caught up in them, in order to safeguard both their finances and their public image.

Someday, we may look back and wonder why these cases existed at all.

We Can Band Together

There is safety and power in numbers. If we —not only victims, not only women, but anyone who wants to further human rights— band together, we can beat sexual harassment. When faced with sexual harassment in the workplace, talk to others: chances are good that if it is happening to you, it has happened to someone else. You shouldn't need backup, but the reality is that if more than one person complains, the complaints will be taken more seriously and handled more quickly than if only one person steps forth.

By the same token, if you have not been sexually harassed but have knowledge—or witnessed—that someone else has been—take that step toward the victim and offer support. Fight that impulse to become an aider and abettor by remaining silent. If you know it to be true, and can find the courage in your heart, align yourself with the victim. Do it for her; do it for yourself. You may be next. The chain of harassment can be broken if we all pull together.

Something else victims can do together is to turn a negative into a positive. If you have gone through sexual harassment—whether you have taken your case public or buried it in the recesses of your soul, whether you have won your case or lost—you have something vital to offer others: you have been there. You are fully qualified to lend an empathetic ear and a sympathetic shoulder to others going through it. That's the best comfort you can offer someone else. Reach out; join a support group such as ASH; offer your services to a hotline. Join the healing process, for others as well as for yourself.

The last piece of good news I have been stressing all along. Eliminating sexual harassment is part of making the world a better place for our children, and we are doing just that.

In the best of all possible worlds, we wouldn't disrespect or take advantage of one another. As our children soak up that message, society will change. If we teach our children to respect each other and themselves, we will help create a healthier workplace for all those who have yet to enter. Respect for all others may seem an impossibly idealistic goal, but surely it is worth working toward, each in our own small way. And that is a worthy legacy.

A Note on Resources

Many resources are available for learning more about sexual harassment. Informative articles have appeared in major newspapers and newsmagazines. Go to the library and ask how to look up recent articles and books on the subject.

Laws about sexual harassment vary from state to state and change constantly. To find out about the laws in your state, contact your local branch of the American Civil Liberties Union. Ask these questions:

1. What is the name of the state agency (not the EEOC) that handles sexual harassment complaints?
2. What is the statute of limitations in your state (the length of time you have to file a claim from the last episode of sexual harassment)?
3. What type of claim can you file in your state?
4. What documentation will you need to bring when you file?

Some organizations that may be helpful in providing information and support are: the Legal Aid Society and the EEOC (Equal Employment Opportunity Commission). Both have local and national chapters.

Finally, there is my organization, ASH (Association for the Sexually Harassed): P.O. Box 27235, Philadelphia, Penn. 19128. (215) 482–3528.

I wish you the very best of luck!

About the Authors

CHERYL GOMEZ-PRESTON, a recognized leader in the field of sexual harassment liability, is a retired veteran Detroit police officer as well as the founder and executive director of the Association for the Sexually Harassed (ASH). As a management-training consultant, she has worked with attorneys and their clients to prepare for trial. She has also mediated disputes within state agencies, helping the participants to avoid litigation. She has advised people internationally through telephone counseling on radio shows on the topic of sexual harassment, and shared her expertise through lectures, workshops, and journal articles. Her television appearances include Oprah Winfrey, Sally Jesse Raphael, CNN, Lifetime, Black Entertainment TV, "People Are Talking," "Kelly & Co.," and many other programs.

RANDI REISFELD is an editor and author who has written about a variety of subjects. Books published include *The Bar/Bat Mitzvah Survival Guide (Citadel Press); The Stars of Beverly Hills, 90210: Their Lives & Loves; Loving Luke: The Luke Perry Story* (Bantam); *Marky Mark and The Funky Bunch* (Avon); and *So You Want to Be a Star: A Teenager's Guide to Breaking Into Showbiz* (Archway). She contributed to the autobiographies of *New Kids on the Block* (Bantam) and *Vanilla Ice* (Avon). In addition, she is editorial director of *16* magazine, and a regular free-lance contributor to Scholastic Publications as well as Great Britain's *Big!* magazine. Her articles have appeared in the *New York Times* and *Women's World* magazine.